# FAITH
# BEYOND
# REASON

# FAITH BEYOND REASON

## A. W. TOZER

EDITED BY GERALD B. SMITH

**STL Books**

**Bromley, Kent**

**Kingsway Publications**

**Eastbourne**

Copyright © Christian Publications 1970

First published in the USA by Christian Publications,
3825 Hartzdale Drive, Camp Hill, PA 17011

First British edition 1987

**British Library Cataloguing in Publication Data**

Tozer, A. W.
    Faith beyond reason: ten sermons from the
Gospel of John.
1. Bible. N. T. John – Commentaries
2. Faith – Biblical teaching
I. Title II. Smith, Gerald B.
            234'.2
            BS2615.3


        STL    ISBN 1 85078 025 0
    Kingsway    ISBN 0 86065 546 6




STL Books are published by Send The Light
(Operation Mobilisation), PO Box 48, Bromley, Kent, England

Published jointly with Kingsway Publications Ltd,
Lottbridge Drive, Eastbourne, E. Sussex, BN23 6NT

Typesetting, production and printing by
Nuprint Ltd, Harpenden, Herts, AL5 4SE

# Contents

# 1

# As Many As Received Him

John 1:11–13   *He came unto his own, and his own received him not. But as many as received him, to them gave he power to become the sons of God, even to them that believe on his name: which were born, not of blood, nor of the will of man, but of God.*

This is an explosive text, teaching as it does about a mysterious, invisible birth – a mystic birth. It cannot be properly handled without getting into areas that some may consider radical. It cannot be handled without considering the fact that there are many people in the world who are God's *creatures* but not God's *children*.

It cannot be handled without an admission that we do truly believe in the Fatherhood of God and the brotherhood of man – stay with me and see what the Word of God says.

It cannot be handled without considering the refusal of many 'believing' Christians to accept the terms of true discipleship – the willingness to turn our backs on everything worldly for Jesus' sake.

It cannot be handled without discussing the fact that receiving Jesus Christ as Saviour and Lord must be an aggressive act of the total personality and not a passive 'acceptance' that makes a door-to-door salesman of the Saviour.

And it certainly cannot be handled without a warning that evangelical Christianity is on a dead-end street if it is going to continue to accept religious activity as a legitimate proof of spirituality.

Now, in this passage, I think it is significant that God informs us about certain people being born, and here is our clue. God has stepped out of His way to talk about certain persons being born, and we know that He never does anything that is merely routine – everything He does is alive, meaningful and brilliantly significant. Why should the great God Almighty, who rounded the earth in the hollow of His hand, who set the sun shining in the heavens and flung the stars to the farthest corner of the night – why should this God take important lines in the Bible record to talk about people being born?

There is much for us to consider here, for we generally consider human birth a very ordinary thing. There are so many babies born in this world every day that it isn't any great thing – except to the parents! But, the only way to get into this world is to be born. There isn't any use to come around with that blarney about sliding down a sunbeam or the stork winging his way over the meadows; all of us have been born at least once!

Our Lord Jesus Christ was one of the most downright realistic teachers that ever lived, and here the Scripture speaks about humans being 'born of the will of the flesh' (the biological urge that is behind every birth) and 'the will of man' (the social arrangement whereby people marry and get social approval). The Word refers also to those born of blood; we are born of blood and our birth has to do with blood and bones and all the rest. That's the level of life upon which we are born.

I once read an allegedly funny little script on a tram ticket. Because she had no scale, a young mother took her baby to the butcher shop, and said, 'Mr Schmidt, I would like to have you weigh Junior for me.' So, he weighed

Junior and handed him back, and said, 'Thirteen pounds mit da bone!' (That was supposed to be funny and I thought I would throw it in!) But the idea is that we are born, and there are bones and blood and flesh and tissue and hair and hide and gristle when we are born into this world.

So, there is no great news particularly in someone's being born, and yet here is God, turning aside and inspiring an apostle to talk about it. He has it recorded by divine inspiration in the Book, preserved at great cost of blood and tears and toil and prayers and hard work for nearly 2,000 years, and gives it to us in familiar English. It is a message that certain people are born, and the reason that it is significant and not ordinary is that these are born of a mystic birth, having nothing whatsoever to do with this common birth of which we know. He says plainly that it is a birth on another level; it isn't on the blood level. He says that it is a birth that doesn't have anything to do with blood, or bones, or tissue. It is a birth that does not have behind it the urge of the flesh. It is a birth that does not have behind it the social arrangement or the will of man or the desire of parents for children.

This invisible birth of which he speaks is an *act of God*. He is talking about something beyond the physical birth that we know. The senses can touch the physical birth. When we were born into this world, the senses could get to us. Those around could see us and touch us and hold us and weigh us, wash and clothe and feed us. But this invisible, mysterious birth of which he speaks has nothing to do with the flesh; it is of heaven. This birth is of the Spirit – a birth of another kind, a mystic birth.

Some people are very greatly perturbed when a preacher uses the word 'mystic'. They want to chase him out immediately and replace him with a man who is just as much afraid of the word as they are. I am not afraid of the word 'mystic' because the whole Bible is a mystical book, a book of mystery, a book of wonder. I have discovered that you can't trace any simple phenomenon back very far without coming up against mystery and darkness, and it is much more so up on the spiritual level.

These of whom the apostle speaks were born of a mystic birth, a birth of the spirit, contrary altogether from any kind of birth that any man knew in the physical sense. If Jesus our Lord merely talked about people being born into the world, He would never have been heard and His teachings would not have got into print, and they would not have been preserved. It is too common – everyone is born. But these people were born of a birth that was not of the body but of the heart. They were born not into time but into eternity. They were born not of earth but of heaven. It was an inward birth, a spiritual birth, a mysterious birth, a mystic birth!

This invisible birth is also a *particular grant* of God.

Now, I know there is a sense in which the sovereign God is over all. I like to think that there isn't a child born anywhere in the world that God doesn't own as His creature. One of our philosophers has said that there are no illegitimate children – only illegitimate parents. In this sense, even those who are born without benefit of clergy or the formalities of the wedding are nevertheless owned by God Almighty as His creatures. But that is down on the level of nature, and it isn't what our Lord was talking about when He said: 'You must be born again.'

This other birth – this mysterious, spiritual birth – was by a particular grant; it was altogether other than, different from, and superior to the first kind of birth. This new birth is a birth that gives an unusual right – the right to be born into the Father's household and thus become the children of God.

Now, when I say here that I believe in the *fatherhood of God* and the *brotherhood of man*, some of you will proceed to faint, and the ushers will kindly be around with an ammonia bottle! You may see fires in men's eyes when they talk about the fatherhood of God and the brotherhood of man, but I believe in both.

That is, I believe that God is the Father of all that believe and thus there is a fatherhood of God. He is the Father by whom the whole family in heaven and earth is named, but He is not the Father of the sinner. I do not foolishly stretch that fatherhood to cover all mankind, for God is not the Father of murderers and the whoremongers. God is the Father of those who believe, and I am not going to let the liberal and the modernist chase me out and run me down an alley and back me up against the wall and make me deny the fatherhood of God.

Furthermore, I believe in the brotherhood of man. God has made of one blood all people that dwell upon the face of the earth, so that all who are born into the world are born of the same blood. Our skins may be different and our eyes slope in different directions. Some will have red hair and some black, some curly and some straight. We may differ from each other greatly in appearance, but there is nevertheless a vast human brotherhood – all of us descended from that man Adam whose mortal sin brought death and all of its fruits into the world.

But it must also be said that there is another brotherhood within that brotherhood – and that is the *brotherhood of the saints of God*, for the fact that there is a broad human brotherhood does not mean that all men are saved. They are not. Not until they are saved, born again, do they leave the old brotherhood of Adam and enter into the brotherhood of the redeemed.

This is where the liberal and the modernist make their mistake – insisting that because mankind is a brotherhood we are all the children of one Father, and therefore we are all saved. That is nonsense; it is unscriptural and it is not true!

I disagree with the liberal who wants to reduce everyone

to a single level – Christian and non-Christian, religious
and irreligious, saved and lost, the believer and the
doubter. When the liberal says he believes in the
fatherhood of God, he isn't believing it in the sense in
which the Bible teaches it.

I believe that there is a brotherhood of man which
comes by the first birth, and another brotherhood which
comes through the second birth. By the grace of God, I
want to dwell in that sacred, mystic brotherhood of the
ransomed and the redeemed, that fellowship of the saints
gathered around the broken body and the shed blood of
the Saviour!

So, it is a mysterious birth and it gives us a particular
privilege. 'As many as received him, to them gave he
power to become the children of God.' The word 'power'
in this verse does not mean dynamics, for it doesn't take
any dynamic power on the part of a man to become a child
of God. It is a gift – He gives us the privilege, the legal
right to become the children of God. This is what is meant
by a man being born into the kingdom of God. The Bible
actually says that God has given us the privilege of being
born, and this is not just poetry. Sometimes we use a
poetic phrase and you have to edit it down and squeeze
the water out of it, as well as the air, and get it down to a
germ of truth to find out what it means. But this is not
poetry – this is theology – 'He gave them the power to
have the right to be the children of God!' In the light of
this, we can understand why they merited the news item,
why they got the by-line, why God Almighty put it in His
news that certain people were born in a special way, not
born just after the flesh. These were the privileged; they
had a right given to them that didn't belong to others – the
right that they should become the children of God.

So, it is plain that a person who is a creature of God
becomes a child of God only when he is born by a special
privilege or right and grant of God Almighty. It should be

of interest to us that this is a right and privilege that even the angels do not have. Actually, there is a time coming when Christian believers will no longer feel like saluting before any broad-winged angel in heaven. The Scripture does tell us that God has made Jesus for a little time lower than the angels, that He might taste death for every man. But originally, Jesus was not lower than angels, because it is written that 'all the angels of God worshipped him'.

The promise to us is this: what Jesus is, we will be. Not in a sense of deity, certainly, but in all the rights and privileges and in standing we will be equal to Him and like Him, for we shall see Him as He is. In that day, if there is any saluting and bowing to be done, the angels will do it, for the children of the Most High God have the high grant and privilege given to them.

Why don't we actually believe that? We don't half believe it! If we did, we would begin to act like it, in preparation for the great day. In England, Prince Charles has been in training and preparation to become the king. He is undergoing a special education, for they have told him, 'You are royal stuff!' I cannot understand why we don't begin to act like children of God if we believe that we have a special higher right to be children of God. We have a right to be sick inside when we see children of heaven acting like the sons of earth, acting like children of the world and the flesh, living like Adam and yet saying that they believe in a new birth by His Spirit.

Now, how did these persons get that privilege? They *believed*, and they *received*. I am going to skip the 'believe' part of it, because we have 'believed' ourselves into a blind alley in many cases. Many who go around 'believing' never really get very much; but these born ones, these born of the mystic birth, believed, in that they were not cynics nor doubters nor pessimists. They took an optimistic, humble, trusting attitude towards Jesus Christ as their Lord and Saviour. They received Him, and to as many as received Him, He gave the power.

You must note that this word 'receive' is not passive. Passive is when I receive the action; active is when I perform the act. I think we have come to the religion of passivity in our day. Toward God, everyone is passive. So we receive Christ; we make it passive!

But the Bible knows absolutely nothing about passive reception, for the word 'receive' is not passive; it is active. We make the word receive into 'accept'. Everyone goes around saying, 'Will you accept Him? Will you accept Him?' This makes a brush salesman out of Jesus Christ, as though He meekly stands waiting to know whether we will patronise Him or not. Although we desperately need what He proffers, we are sovereignly deciding whether we will receive Him or not.

Let me repeat that passive reception is unknown in the Bible. There is no hint of it within the confines of sacred writ. I for one am tired of being told what to believe by people who copy everybody else just like parrots. You could put some of the ministers on perches and they would say 'Polly wants a cracker! Good morning!' all in the same tone of voice. If anyone challenges their line in their books and magazines and songs, they look over their religious noses at you and declare that you are either radical or touched with modernism.

The simple fact is that we have been taught that passive acceptance is equivalent to faith, when it is not. In the Greek this word 'receive' is active – not passive. You can go to any of the modern translations and you will find out that they get across the idea of 'take' and 'took'. 'As many as took him,' says one fine translation, 'to them gave he the power to become the sons of God.'

It is the 'taking' instead of 'accepting,' and I want you to take this thought down, whether you are layman or minister, missionary or student: receiving Christ savingly is an act of the total personality. It is an act of the mind and of the will and of the affections, and it is thus not only an act of the total personality; it is an *aggressive* act of the total personality. Therefore, when you bring this thought over into this text, the Holy Spirit is saying of the children of God: 'As many as aggressively took Him with their total personality.' There is no inference that they could sit and quietly accept. Every part of the being became a hand reaching forth for Jesus Christ. They took Jesus Christ as Saviour and Lord with all of their will and all of their affections and all of their feelings and all of their intellect. That's why it says in the Greek: 'As many as took Him actively.'

Evangelical Christianity is gasping for breath, for we happen to have come upon us a period when it is a popular thing to sing about tears and prayers and believing. You can get a religious phrase kicked around almost anywhere right in the middle of a worldly programme dedicated to the world, the flesh and the devil. Old Mammon, with two silver dollars for eyes, sits at the top of it, lying about the quality of the products, shamelessly praising actors who ought to be put to work laying bricks. In the middle of it, someone will say with an unctuous voice, trained in a studio to sound religious, 'Now, our hymn for the week!' So they break in, and the band goes 'Twinkle, twankle, twinkle, twankle'; and they sing something that the devil must blush to hear. They call that religion, and I will admit that, all right, but it isn't salvation and it isn't Christianity and it isn't the Holy Ghost. It isn't New Testament and it isn't redemption; it is simply making capital out of religion for a price.

I still believe, however, that if someone should come along who could make himself heard to thousands instead of to a few hundred, someone with as much oil as intellect and as much power as penetration, we could yet save evangelical Christianity from the dead-end street in which she finds herself. I warn you: don't for one second let the crowds, the bustle of religious activity, a surge of religious thinking, fool you into thinking that there is a lot of spirituality. It isn't so.

That's why the meaning of the word 'took' is so important here: as many as took Him, actively and aggressively took Him. This means a determined exercise of the will that will not deny any condition that the Lord lays down. You hear me now? That is something quite different from what we are hearing. They did not come to the Lord and try to make terms but they came to the Lord and actively took Him on His own terms.

This is the child of God, the believer in Christ who will meet any condition the Lord lays down, even to the forsaking of relatives and friends. 'Oh, you are getting radical again,' you say. 'We knew you couldn't preach one sermon that didn't have some radical statements in it.' Well, maybe so, but did you ever read the words of Jesus in the passage that says: 'If any man comes to me and hates not father and mother and husband and wife, and yea, his children, and his very life also, he cannot be my disciple'?

We have edited Jesus Christ down. We get bitter and fight over translations; but any modern translation will tell you that Jesus Christ said, 'If you don't come to me and love me beyond all your family, you can't be my disciple. If you are not willing to place love for me, your Saviour, before that of love for wife, or husband, or children, I won't have you. If you are not willing to forsake your father, or mother, for my sake, I won't have you.'

That's the sum of the teaching of Jesus on this subject. 'It is cruel – terribly cruel,' you say. The living God demands our love and our loyalty, and we look upon it as cruelty! Actually, hell is so hot that God is still doing all that He can to arouse us and stir us into action. Lot could have been justified if he had forsaken that ungodly family of his and gone out alone from Sodom.

Let's get it straight. Jesus Christ doesn't just offer us salvation as though it is a decoration or a bouquet or some addition to our garb. He says plainly: 'Throw off your old rags – strip to the skin! Let me dress you in the fine clean robes of my righteousness – all mine. Then, if it means loss of money, lose it! If it means loss of job, lose it! If it means persecution will come, take it! If it brings the stiff winds of opposition, bow your head into the wind and take it – for Jesus' sake!'

To receive Jesus Christ as Lord is not a passive, soft affair – not a pre-digested kind of religion. It is strong meat, brethren. It is such strong meat that God is calling us in this hour to yield everything to Him. Some want to cling to their sinful pleasures, and in our churches in this deadly, degenerate, sodomistic hour, we are guilty of making it just as easy as possible for double-minded Christians.

'Just believe on Jesus and accept Him, and then you can be as you were before, you can do what you did before, as long as you don't get drunk and run after women. Everything else is all right. Amen!' This is the kind of marginal Christianity that is being passed along in too many circles, and the result is that we have a religion that is not much better than Buddhism or Zoroastrianism. I think I would rather follow Zoroaster and kneel twice a day to the rising and setting sun than to be a half-baked Christian who insists upon 'believing' for salvation, and then doing as he pleases and violating the lordship of the Saviour.

You can't do it, brethren, even if it is a popular idea in our day to give them something to make them happy and tell them that they can get to heaven. Tell them they can get eternal life and never lose it, just by 'accepting', and after that they can do as they please! You can have big conferences built on that – even Bible schools and colleges and great groups of busy Christians – all built around this erroneous idea. But the Bible says that as many as 'took' Him, took Him aggressively, with their whole personality.

Shakespeare had Hamlet say, 'Denmark – all of Denmark is contracted in one great brow of woe.' I would like to change that and say, 'All of the human personality is contracted in one grasping of an aggressive hand that reaches out and takes Jesus and says, 'Here, Lord, You are mine – if it costs me blood and death. You are mine – if it costs me the loss of friendships. You are mine – if it means the loss of job or position or standing!'

It can be illustrated often within our own group. I think of the late Louis Henry Zeimer of Toledo, pastor of one of our largest and most influential congregations for many years prior to his death. Before his conversion, he was the minister of a denominational church. He often told of reading a copy of *The Alliance Weekly* for the first time, and how he came face to face with the possibility that he could be saved – and know it. Simply, he gave his heart to the Lord and was converted. Then he began to preach to his people about the wonder of the new birth and the revivals came. He was called to account by the leaders of his denomination, so he got up and read to them from Luther's writings and showed them that he was preaching what Luther had taught about faith and justification. They cleared him, but asked him to resign. Brother Zeimer said: 'That was a promotion!' He accepted the pulpit of a small Alliance church (in those days we were usually behind a horse stable or over a barber shop) but his preaching and his ministry brought it up into the great Toledo Tabernacle that has sent scores of missionaries around the world, even three of his own sons and daughters on the mission field. This man knew what it was to receive and live for Christ aggressively with his total personality. He gave up everything. They threw him out of the denomination! Away went pulpits, parsonages, pensions;

all of that went for Christ's sake.

Lesser men and women say: 'That is cruel!' But what of the Communists? Communists dedicate themselves to the cause of Communism; they are willing to give their very lives to support their faith in their doctrines of world revolution. In the light of that, why should anyone charge God with cruelty when He offers me eternal life through Jesus Christ, heaven and all the glories that lie beyond, with the expectation that I will be willing to turn my back on everything else as a child of God? Nothing cruel about it at all. Why should believing Christians want everything pre-cooked, pre-digested, sliced and salted, and expect that God must come and help us eat and hold the food to our baby lips while we pound the table and splash? And we think that is Christianity! Brethren, it is not. It is a degenerate illegitimate breed that has no right to be called Christianity.

The human being who insists that the Lord God 'toady' to him, letting him continue on as he is going, and still say to him in the end, 'Come, thou faithful servant,' is a moral fool.

Someone ought to tell him so now. I would like to be the fellow to tell him!

# 2

# Revelation Is Not Enough

John 7:14–17  *About the midst of the feast, Jesus went up into the temple, and taught; and the Jews marvelled, saying, How knoweth this man letters, having never learned? Jesus answered them and said, My doctrine is not mine, but His that sent me. If any man will do His will, he shall know the doctrine, whether it be of God, or whether I speak of myself.*

I think Jesus has given us reason in this passage to take a look at those in His day who held truth to be intellectual merely, capable of being reduced to a code. Their thought about truth was that it was an intellectual thing – just as we know and accept that two times two is four.

This philosophy of truth held in Jesus' day will also lead us into a necessary consideration of those who cling to an intellectual concept of God's truth in our own times. I refer not to the theological liberals who deny the person and the position of Jesus Christ as the Son of God; I refer rather to those whom I must call the evangelical rationalists of our own day. The reason for my concern in bringing this pointed message to you is my conclusion that evangelical rationalism will kill the truth just as quickly as liberalism will.

First, let us take a look at these Jewish leaders in Jesus'

day. They marvelled at Him, and they said to one another,
'How does this man know letters, having never learned?'
It was their thought that Jesus had never studied in the
accepted schools of higher learning. I think most of the
schools in those days consisted of a rabbi coming and
teaching little groups, rather than having colleges and
schools as we know them now. Our Lord had evidently
never attended that kind of rabbinical school, so they
said, 'How does He get His wonderful doctrine, seeing
that He has never been to the schools of the rabbis?'

Now, this question alone tells us a good deal about
them. It tells us that they held truth (and you can spell it
with capital letters if you please) to be intellectual merely,
capable of being reduced to a code. Then, to know truth,
it was only necessary to learn and memorise the code.
Most of them had no books of their own; they memorised
the code in school and so held it in their memory, and this
was their concept of truth. We gather this not only from
verse 17 but from the entire Gospel of John.

Their thought about truth was that it was an intellectual
thing. With us, the fact that two times two is four is truth,
but it is an intellectual truth – proof to the mind. All you
have to do is learn the multiplication table up to two times
two and you've got that. They had reduced divine truth to
that status. To them, there was no mysterious depth in
truth, nothing beneath and nothing beyond – two times
two made four. It was exactly here that they parted
company with our Saviour, for the Lord Jesus constantly
taught the 'beyond' and the 'beneath'. But they could
never sense the depth of His teaching – they only saw that
two times two made four.

It is this that we must remember: those religious leaders
evidently believed that the *words* of truth are the truth,
and this is still a basic misunderstanding of Christian
theology. To make this analysis in our own day is not just
a matter of splitting hairs. Oh, no! If it were only splitting

hairs, I wouldn't bother, but it has both moral and spiritual consequences. They believed that the *word* of truth was truth – that if you had the words, you had the truth. If you could repeat the code of truth, you had the truth. If you were living by the word of truth, you were living in the truth.

I repeat that this is exactly where they had parted company with our Lord Jesus Christ.

The Saviour tried to correct this inadequate view. He showed them the heavenly quality of His message. He showed them that He was simply a transparent medium through which God spoke. He said, 'My doctrine is not mine – I am not a rabbi just teaching doctrine that you can memorise and repeat. What I am giving you is not that kind of doctrine at all.'

He had said previously, 'I say nothing for myself – what I see the Father do, that I do, and what the Father speaks, that I speak. What I have seen yonder I tell you about. I am a transparent medium through which the truth is being spoken. You believe that the way to truth is to go to a rabbi and learn it, but that is not the truth – that approach to truth is inadequate.'

Here, it seems to me, is the weakness in modern Christianity, and I am wondering why there is so much silence about it. The battle line, the warfare today, is not necessarily between the fundamentalist and the liberal. There is a difference between them, of course. The fundamentalist says, 'God made the heaven and the earth.' The liberal says, 'Well, that is a poetic way of stating it – but actually, it came up by evolution.'

The fundamentalist says, 'Jesus Christ is the very Son of God.' The liberal replies, 'Well, He certainly was a wonderful man and He is the Master, but I don't quite know about His deity.' So, there is a division, but I don't think the warfare is on these matters anymore.

Some years ago I went to Gettysburg with friends, and

we fought again in review the famous battle of the Civil War. We read the plaques and memorials, but there is no fighting there; I heard no boom of cannons, I saw no dead soldiers, I heard no clash of swords; I only saw where the battle had taken place.

Now in our day, there are still a few ministers waving their bloody swords over their heads; but the blood is dry, for there is really no fresh blood between liberalism and fundamentalism. It has been settled; those who are liberals are liberals, and those who are fundamentalists know what they believe and where they stand – but the fight isn't there. The battle has shifted to another and more important field.

The warfare, the dividing line today, is between evangelical *rationalists* and evangelical *mystics*. I will explain what I mean.

There is today an *evangelical rationalism* which is the same as these Jews had. They said the truth is in the word, and if you want to know the truth, go to the rabbi and learn the word. If you get the word, you have got the truth. That is evangelical rationalism and we have that today in fundamental circles as big as a sheep (as my grandmother used to say; I don't know why she used the expression!). We have it among us. It is a doctrine that 'if you learn the text you've got the truth'.

This evangelical rationalism will kill the truth just as quickly as liberalism will, though in a more subtle way. The liberal stands over there and says in frankness: 'I don't believe your inspired Bible; I don't believe your deified Christ. I believe the Bible in a way; it is the record of high points of great men and I believe in a certain mystic communion with the universe and it is all very wonderful, but I don't believe as you do.' You can easily spot this man; train your glasses on him and there he stands. You can tell he is on the other side, for he wears the uniform of the other side.

But the evangelical rationalist today is still wearing our uniform. He comes right in wearing our uniform and says what the Pharisees said while Jesus was on earth, and they were His worst enemies: 'Well, truth is truth, and if you believe the truth you've got it!'

In His day or in our day, such see no beyond and no mystic depth, no mysterious heights, nothing supernatural or divine. They see only 'I believe in God the Father Almighty, Maker of heaven and earth: and in Jesus Christ His only Son, our Lord.' They have the text and the code and the creed, and to them, that is the truth. So they pass it on to others. The result is we are dying spiritually.

Now, what about the *evangelical mystic*? I don't really like the word 'mystic' because you think of a fellow with long hair and a little goatee who acts dreamy and strange. Maybe it is not a good word at all, but I am talking about the spiritual side of things – that the truth is more than the text. There is something that you've got to get through to. The truth is more than the code. There is a heart beating in the middle of the code and you've got to get there.

The important question is simply this: *Is the body of Christian truth enough*? Or, does truth have a soul as well as a body? The evangelical rationalist says that all of that talk about the soul of truth is poetic nonsense. The body of truth is all you need; if you believe the body of truth you are on your way to heaven and you can't backslide and everything will be all right and you will get a crown in the last day.

Now otherwise stated: *Is revelation enough or must there be illumination?* Is this Bible an inspired book? Is it a revealed book? Of course you and I believe that it is a revelation, that God spoke all these words and holy men spoke as they were moved by the Holy Ghost.

I believe that this Bible is a living book, that God has given it to us and that we dare not add to it or take away from it. It is revelation.

But *revelation is not enough!* There must be illumination before revelation can get to your soul. It is not enough that I hold an inspired book in my hands. I must have an inspired heart. There is the difference, in spite of the evangelical rationalist who insists that revelation is enough.

These things are happening in North America today. A minister came to see me recently, and told me of his experiences with a church group in the south. They believe truth is enough, the code is enough. Those who come and say, 'I believe in Christ,' are taken into the church and no questions asked. They are in. This brother had a moving, spiritual experience in his own life, with floods of glory coming down and the wings of love beating over his soul as they did over Christians in evangelist Finney's day. He tells me that he has been invited 'out' of his denomination, attacked by men whose only accusation against him is his belief in the miraculous, divine element of grace. He believes not only in the revelation of God's grace in the book – he believes that the new birth is a miraculous act of God within the soul.

Who attacked him and accused him of heresy? The *fundamentalists* did, my brother. The evangelicals did – the evangelical rationalists who say, 'If you but believe, everything is all right.' And they did it in Jesus' day, too, when they said, 'How about this man? He never sat at the rabbi's feet and memorised the text. He doesn't have the truth!'

You can memorise all of the texts of the Bible – and I believe in memorising – but when you are through, you've got nothing but the body. There is the *soul* of truth as well as the body. There is a divine inward illumination the Holy Ghost must give us or we don't know what the truth means.

*There* is the difference. We must insist that conversion is a miraculous act of God by the Holy Ghost; it must be wrought in the spirit. The body of truth, the inspired text, is not enough; there must be an inward illumination!

In His day, Christ's conflict was with the theological rationalist. It revealed itself in the Sermon on the Mount and in the whole book of John. Just as Colossians argues against Manichaeism and Galatians argues against Jewish legalism, so the Book of John is a long, inspired, passionately outpoured book trying to save us from evangelical rationalism, the doctrine that says the text is enough. Textualism is as deadly as liberalism.

Now revelation, I repeat, cannot save. Revelation is the ground upon which we stand. Revelation tells us what to believe. It is the book of God and I stand for it with all my heart; but there must be, before I can be saved, illumination, penitence, renewal, inward deliverance.

I have no doubt that we try to ease many people into the kingdom, so called, who never get into the kingdom at all. They are jockeyed into believing in the text, and they do, but they have never been illuminated by the Holy Ghost. They have never been renewed within their beings. They never get into the kingdom at all.

Now, there is a secret in divine truth altogether hidden from the unprepared souls. This is where we stand in the terrible day in which we live. Christianity is not something you just reach up and grab, as some are taught. There must be a preparation of the mind, a preparation of the life and a preparation of the inner man before we can savingly believe in Jesus Christ.

Somebody asks, Is it possible to hear the truth and not understand the truth? Listen to Isaiah: 'Hear ye indeed, but understand not; and see ye indeed, but perceive not' (6:9). It is possible to see yet not perceive. Paul says (1 Cor. 2:4, 5): 'My speech and my preaching was not with enticing words of man's wisdom, but in demonstration of the Spirit and of power: that your faith should not stand in the wisdom of men, but in the power of God.'

Now the theological rationalist understands that in this

way: he says that your faith should stand not in the wisdom of man but in the Word of God. But that is not what Paul said. He said that your faith should stand in the *power* of God. That is quite a different thing.

Verses 9 to 14 say: 'Eye hath not seen nor ear heard, neither have entered into the heart of man, the things which God hath prepared for them that love him. But God hath revealed them unto us by his Spirit: for the Spirit searcheth all things, yea, the deep things of God. For what man knoweth the things of man, save the spirit of man which is in him? even so the things of God knoweth no man, but the Spirit of God...But the natural man receiveth not the things of the Spirit of God: for they are foolishness unto him: neither can he know them, because they are spiritually discerned.'

Paul, the man of God, is saying: I came preaching and I preached with power that would illuminate and get to the conscience and to the spirit and change the inner man in order that your faith might stand in the power of God.

My brethren, your faith can stand in the text and you can be as dead as the proverbial doornail, but when the power of God moves in on the text and sets the sacrifice on fire, then you have Christianity. We try to call that revival, but it is not revival at all. It is simply New Testament Christianity. It is what it ought to have been in the first place and was not.

Now look at Matthew 11: 'Jesus answered and said, I thank thee, O Father, Lord of heaven and earth, because thou hast hid these things from the wise and prudent, and hast revealed them unto babes. Even so, Father: for so it seemed good in thy sight. All things are delivered unto me of my Father: and no man knoweth the Son, but the Father; neither knoweth any man the Father, save the Son, and he to whomsoever the Son will reveal him.'

So there we have the doctrine taught plainly that there is not only a body of truth which we must hold at our peril

– there is also a soul in that body which we must get through to, and if we don't get through to the soul of truth, we have only a dead body on our hands.

A church can go on holding the creed and the truth for years and generations and grow old and die and new people come up and receive that same code and they grow old and die. Then some revivalist comes in and fires his guns and gets everybody stirred, and prayer moves God down on the scene and revival comes to that church. People who thought they were saved get saved. People who have only believed in a code now believe in Christ. And what has really happened? It is simply New Testament Christianity having its place. It is not any deluxe edition of Christianity – it is what it should have been in the first place.

A man will go along in a church and believe texts and quote them and memorise them and teach them and maybe become a deacon. He may be elected to the church board, and all the rest. Then one day under the fiery preaching of some visitor or maybe the pastor, he suddenly feels himself terribly in need of God and he forgets all his past history and goes to his knees and like David begins to pour out his soul in confession. Then he leaps to his feet and testifies, 'I have been a deacon in this church for twenty-six years and never was born again until tonight.'

What happened? That man had been trusting the dead body of truth until some inspired preacher let him know that truth has a soul. Or maybe God taught him in secret that truth has a soul as well as a body and he dared to get through and pursue by penitence and obedience until God honoured his faith and flashed the light on. Then like lightning out of heaven it touched his spirit and all the texts he had memorised became alive.

Thank God, he did memorise the texts, and all the truth he knew suddenly now bloomed in the light. That is why I believe we ought to memorise. That is why we ought to get to know the Word, why we ought to fill our minds with the songs and the great hymns of the church. They won't mean anything to us until the Holy Ghost comes. But when He comes He will have fuel to use. Fire without fuel won't burn but fuel without fire is dead. And the Holy Ghost will not come on a church where there is no biblical fuel. There must be Bible teaching. We must have the body of truth. The Holy Ghost never comes into a vacuum, but where the Word of God is, there is fuel, and the fire falls and burns up the sacrifice.

Jesus said if any man is willing to do God's will, he shall *know*; he shall know the *doctrine*. Now, this body of truth can be grasped by the average, normal intellect. You can grasp truth, but only the enlightened soul will ever know the truth and only the prepared heart will ever be enlightened. And just what is the preparation needed?

Jesus said, 'If any man is willing to do My will the light will flash in on him. If any man will obey Me God will enlighten his soul immediately.' We make Jesus Christ a convenience. We make Him a lifeboat to get us to shore, a guide to find us when we are lost. We reduce Him simply to Big Friend to help us when we are in trouble. That is not biblical Christianity. Jesus Christ is Lord, and when a man is willing to do His will, he is repenting, and the truth flashes in. For the first time in his life, he finds himself willing to say, 'I will do the will of the Lord, even if I die for it!' Illumination will start in his heart. That is repentance, my brethren; he has been following his own will and now decides to do the will of God!

No man can know the Son except the Father tell him. No man can know the Father except the Son reveal Him. I can know about God; that's the body of truth. But I can't know God, the soul of truth, unless I am ready to be obedient. True discipleship is obeying Jesus Christ and learning of Him and following Him and doing what He tells you to do, keeping His commandments and carrying out His will. That kind of a person is a Christian – and no other kind is.

And when you are trying to find out the condition of a church, don't just find out whether it is 'fundamentalist'. Find out whether it is an evangelical rationalistic church which says, 'The text is enough,' or whether it is a church that believes that the text plus the Holy Ghost is enough.

Before the Word of God can mean anything inside of me there must be obedience to the Word. Truth will not give itself to a rebel. Truth will not impart life to a man who will not obey the light! 'If we walk in the light, as he is in the light, we have fellowship one with another, and the blood of Jesus Christ his Son cleanseth us from all sin.' If you are disobeying Jesus Christ you can't expect to be enlightened.

But there *is* illumination. I know what Charles Wesley meant when he wrote, 'His Spirit answers to the blood, and tells me I am born of God!' Nobody had to come and tell me what he meant. 'He that is willing to do my will,' said Jesus, 'shall have a revelation in his own heart. He shall have an inward illumination that tells him he is a child of God.'

If a sinner goes to the altar and a worker with a marked New Testament argues him into the kingdom, the devil will meet him two blocks down the street and argue him out of it again. But if he has an inward illumination and he has that witness within because the Spirit answers to the blood, you can't argue with that man. He will just be stubborn, regardless of the arguments you try to bring in. He will say, 'But I know!'

A man like that is not bigoted or arrogant; he is just sure. He is like the happy Christian brother who worked in a factory, and someone invited him to attend a meeting where a man had announced he would argue against the Christian faith, and his lecture would prove that Christians were wrong. So he went to the lecture. It was powerful and buttressed by every kind of argument. On the way out, the man who had invited him said to the Christian brother, 'Now what do you think?' 'Oh, I heard this lecture twenty-five years too late,' the Christian chap replied. 'It was twenty-five years ago that God did for me what this fellow said can't be done!' Now, this is normal Christianity. That's the way we should be. 'If any man will do his will, he shall know.'

Some of us continue to hold out on God, refusing to follow Jesus, all the time hanging up on some point – something He has told us to do and we won't do it. So you can say you are going to take a Bible course. You can take a study course, and learn all about synthesis and analysis and all the rest. But if you are holding out on God, you might just as well read Pogo; all the courses in the world won't illuminate you inside. You can fill your head full of knowledge, but the day that you decide you are going to obey God, it will get down into your heart. You shall know. Only the servants of truth can ever know truth. Only those who obey can ever have the inward change.

You can stand on the outside and have all the information and know all about it and yet not be a true disciple who really knows Christ. I once read a book about the inner spiritual life by a man who was not a Christian at all. He was a sharp intellectual, a keen Englishman. He stood outside and examined spiritual people from the outside, but nothing ever reached him. And that's possible!

You cannot argue around this. You can read your Bible – read any version you want – and if you are honest you will admit that it is either obedience or inward blindness. You can repeat the Book of Romans word for word and still be blind inwardly. You can quote the whole Book of Psalms and still be blind inwardly. You can know the doctrine of justification by faith and take your stand with Luther and the Reformation and be blind inwardly. For it is not the body of truth that enlightens; it is the Spirit of truth that enlightens.

If you are willing to obey the Lord Jesus, He will illuminate your spirit, inwardly enlighten you; and the truth you have known will now be known spiritually, and power will begin to flow up and out and you will find yourself changed, marvellously changed. It is rewarding to believe in a Christianity that really changes men and women.

Well, I would rather have a small group inside than to have the vast numbers and be on the outside. In that great day of Christ's coming, all that will matter is whether or not I have been inwardly illuminated, inwardly regenerated, inwardly purified.

The question is: *Do we really know Jesus in this way?*

# 3

# Faith in the Character of God

*John 14:13, 14  Whatsoever ye shall ask in my name, that will I do; that the Father may be glorified in the Son. If ye shall ask anything in my name, I will do it.*

In our evangelical circles, faith is a theme upon which we like to dwell. Some are concerned because there are not more miracles and wonders wrought in our midst through faith. In our day, everything is commercialised, and I must say that I do not believe in wonders and miracles that are organised and incorporated. 'Miracles, Incorporated' – you can have it! 'Healing, Incorporated,' – you can have that, too! And the same with Evangelism, Incorporated,' and 'Without a Vision the People Perish, Incorporated!' You can have it all. I have my doubts about signs and wonders that have to be organised, that demand a letterhead and a president and a secretary and a big trailer with lights and cameras. God isn't in that!

But the man of faith can go alone into the wilderness and get on his knees and command heaven; God is in that. The man who will dare to stand and let his preaching cost him something; God is in that. The Christian who is willing to put himself in a place where he must get the answer from God and God alone; the Lord is in that!

You know by this time that I have a philosophy of faith,

and I must begin by telling you that I cannot recommend that we have faith in 'faith'. We have a great deal of that kind of thing right now because there are men who are devoted completely to preaching faith. As a result, people have faith in 'faith', and largely forget that our confidence is not in the power of faith but in the person and work of the Saviour, Jesus Christ.

So, I have to confess that I cannot major in preaching that kind of faith; I never have – and, so help me, I will not start it now. I know better.

In 1 John 5, the apostle writes out of divine inspiration: 'This is the confidence we have in him, that, if we ask any thing according to his will, he heareth us: And if we know that he hear us, whatsoever we ask, we know that we have the petitions that we desired of him.'

We have full confidence in Jesus Christ, and that is the origin and source and foundation and resting place for all of our faith. In that kingdom of faith, we are dealing with Him, with God Almighty, the One whose essential nature is holiness, the one who cannot lie. Our confidence rises as the character of God becomes greater and more beautiful and more trustworthy to spiritual comprehension. The One with whom we deal is the One before whom goes faithfulness and truth, the One who cannot lie.

So, this is the confidence we have in Him. Faith mounts up on its long heavenly boots, up the mountain top, up toward the shining peaks, and says in satisfaction 'If God says it, I know it is so!' It is the character of God Himself, you see, that gives us this confidence.

Now, I have to give you another warning here about the great differences today between the evangelical rationalist and the evangelical mystic. There is a great difference between believing God and having confidence in Him because of His character, instead of believing that the things of God can be proved and grasped by human reason. We do have evangelical rationalists now who insist on trying to reduce everything down to where it can be explained and proved, with the result that we are rationalising faith. This is the manner in which we seek to pull Almighty God down to the low level of the human reason.

I am not insisting here that human reason and faith in God lie contrary to one another, but I do insist that one lies above the other. When we are true believers in God's truth we enter another world – a realm that is infinitely above reason. 'My thoughts are not your thoughts nor my ways your ways'; as high as the heavens above the earth, so great are the thoughts of God above the thoughts of men. Faith never goes contrary to reason; faith simply ignores reason and rises above it.

Now, in dealing with these matters in the text, we must first go back the the plain statement of our Lord that 'if ye shall ask anything in my name, I will do it.'

Let me say this to begin: there is a great deal of praying being done among us that does not amount to anything! It is futile and never brings anything back to us. There is no possible good that can come in our trying to cover up or deny it. The truth is that there is enough prayer made on any Sunday to save the whole word—but the world is not saved. About the only thing that comes back after our praying is the echo of our own voice. Brethren, I contend that this kind of praying which is so customary among us has a most injurious effect upon the church of Christ.

If unanswered prayer continues in a congregation over an extended period of time, there will be a chill and discouragement settling over the praying people. If we continue to ask and ask and ask like a petulant child, never expecting to get what it asks for but continuing to whine for it, we will get chilled and cold within our beings.

If we continue in our prayers and never get an answer, it will tend to confirm the natural unbelief of the human heart, for remember this: the human heart by nature is filled with unbelief. It was unbelief and not disobedience which was the first sin. While disobedience was the first recorded sin, behind the act of disobedience there was the sin of unbelief, or the act of disobedience would not have taken place.

The fact of unanswered prayer will also encourage the idea that religion is unreal, and this idea is held by many people in our day. 'Religion is unreal,' they tell us. 'It is a subjective thing completely, and there is nothing real about it.'

It is true that there may be nothing tangible to which it can be referred. If I use the word 'lake', everyone thinks of a large body of water. When I use the word 'star', everyone thinks immediately of a heavenly body. But when we use such words as 'faith' and 'belief' and 'God' and 'heaven' there is not any image of a reality which is known to us and to which our mind immediately refers. To most people those are just words – like 'pixies' and 'fairies'. So, there is a false idea of unreality in our hearts when we pray and pray and pray and receive no answers.

Perhaps worst of all is the fact that our failures in prayer leave the enemy in possession of the field. The worst part about the failure of a military drive is not the loss of men nor the loss of face, but the fact that the enemy is left in possession of the field. In the spiritual sense, this is both a tragedy and a disaster, for the devil ought to be on the run. We should never see anything but the back of his neck. He should always be retreating and fighting a rear guard action. But, instead of that, this blasphemous enemy smugly and scornfully holds his position, and the people of God let him have it. No wonder that the work of the Lord is greatly retarded in many areas.

I repeat, that if we do not have any prayers answered, if our prayers ascend up to heaven and come back empty, it is just like sending an army out to battle without weapons. It is just like sending a woodsman into the woods without an axe. It is like sending a farmer into the field without a plough. Little wonder that the work of God stands still!

Dare we realise that Jesus said that we can have anything that we ask in His name? John emphasises the truth when he says: 'This is the confidence . . . the boldness . . . the assurance that we have.' I am not adding words, for our English language is highly versatile – almost volatile. It is the richest of all the languages because it has received tributaries from everywhere. Our difficulty is that we often would be forced to use a half-dozen words to mean as much as one word means in another language. So, when the Holy Spirit through John says: 'This is the confidence we have in him,' the word 'confidence' is not sufficiently strong in the English, so the translators declare it is 'boldness' that we have in Him. Others say: 'This is the assurance that we have in Him.' So, it takes the words 'confidence', 'boldness' and 'assurance' to express in our minds what John meant when he said, 'This is that which we feel towards Him.'

It is right here that we come to the parting of the ways between the man of faith and the man of reason. This kind of teaching, that we can have confidence in God and he will give us what we ask according to His will, is flatly rejected by the man of unbelief. He says it cannot be so, that he will not accept it, and he demands the proof of human reason.

Now, I must remind you that unbelief is not just a mental attitude – it is a moral thing. Unbelief is always sinful because it always pre-supposes an immoral condition of the heart before it can exist. Unbelief is not the failure of the mind to grasp the truth. It is not the failure or unsoundness of a logical premise. It is not a bad conclusion drawn from a logical premise. It is a moral sin. This man who says that he cannot believe in the promises of God cannot understand this language with which we are dealing here. He says: 'I must have a better reason for believing this than John's record that if we have confidence in God He will hear us and answer us.'

And yet, all of this time as the argument goes on, the man of faith is confident. The man of faith does not dare rest on human reason. He does not reject the place of human reason, but he knows there are things that human reason cannot do.

This is my own personal position: I have never been against human reason. I have only expressed myself against human reason trying to do the things that human reason is not qualified to do. In every area where human reason is qualified, I say, 'Turn human reason loose.' You have a can opener in your house, and reason guides you in its use. In other words, you use the opener on cans, not to mend your little boy's stockings.

Nearly every man has a hammer and a saw in his base-ment work-room. He knows what they are for and how they should be used; he uses them to pound nails and cut boards, but he doesn't use them to paper the walls of the living room!

Everything was created for a purpose and I claim that there are some things that human reason cannot do, things that are beyond its capacity.

Reason could not tell us that Jesus Christ should be born of a virgin, but faith knows that He was. Reason cannot prove that Jesus took upon Him the form of a man and that He died for the sins of the world, but faith knows that He did. Reason cannot prove that on the third day Jesus rose from the dead, but faith knows that He did, for faith is an organ of knowledge. The rationalists take the position that the human brain alone is the organ of know-ledge, but they either forget or overlook completely that feeling is a means of knowledge, and so is faith.

Many of us suffered in today's heat, but all the reason in the world couldn't tell you that the temperature was 98 degrees. You felt that it was, though, didn't you? Feeling is a means of knowledge. A young man loves a young woman. How does he know it? Does he read the encyclopedia in order to base his love on reason? No, he listens to the ticking of his own heart. He knows it by feeling.

So, along with reason, feeling is a means of knowledge, and faith can be placed in the same category. This means that the man who believes and has placed his confidence in God has access to knowledge that the man who merely thinks and reasons cannot have.

Reason cannot say, 'I know that He will come to judge the quick and the dead,' but faith knows that He will come. Reason cannot say, 'My sins are all gone,' but faith knows that they are forgiven and forgotten. Faith simply ignores reason, and rises above it. The brain just comes staggering along behind like a little boy trying to keep up with his dad. The brain, like the little boy, comes along on short, stubby legs, trying to reason.

This is exactly why the word 'wonder' often appears in the New Testament. 'They wondered at him.' 'They wondered at him, and they all marvelled.' Faith was going ahead doing wonders and reason was coming along, wide-eyed and amazed. That is the way it should be, always.

But in our day, we send reason ahead on those little short legs and faith never follows. Nobody marvels because the whole business can be explained. I have always claimed that a believing Christian is a miracle, and at the precise moment that you can fully explain him and all about it, you have a Christian no longer! I have read the efforts of William James to psychologise the wonders of God's workings in the human life and experience, but the real and genuine child of God is someone who cannot be explained by human reasoning.

In this relationship with Jesus Christ through the new birth, something takes place by the ministry of the Spirit of God which psychology cannot explain. This is why I must contend that faith is the highest kind of reason, after all, for faith goes straight into the presence of God. Our Lord Jesus Christ has gone ahead as a forerunner for us, and engages God Almighty on our behalf. It is for this reason alone that man may reach that for which he was created, and finally communes with the source of his being, loving the fountain of his life, praying to the One who has begotten him, and resting in the knowledge that God made heaven and earth.

Now, this redeemed man may not be an astronomer but he knows the God who made the stars. He may not be a physicist but he knows the God who made mathematics. There may be many technical and local bits of knowledge which he does not have, but he knows the God of all knowledge and enters in beyond the veil and into His presence, and there stands hushed and wide-eyed and gazes and gazes upon the wonders of Deity. It is faith that takes him there, and reason cannot disprove anything that faith discovers and knows. Reason can never do that.

Why should Christian writers think that they have to come to the help of Almighty God, supporting the Bible, as they say, by quoting and reconciling a few scientific facts? I tell you they are all going in the wrong direction, but this is what good men are doing. Many of them are better men than I am, but they are wrong. Not all of the scientific facts ever assembled in any university of the world can support one spiritual fact; you are dealing with two different realms. One deals with reason, and the other deals with faith in God. If the sun should begin rising in the west and take its course to the east, and if the summer should end immediately and plunge into the middle of winter without any autumn, and if the corn in the fields started growing down instead of up – none of these things would change my mind about God or the Bible! I haven't the words to emphasise strongly enough my position that faith in God is not dependent upon the support of any scientific helps.

No, we have confidence and boldness in Him because He is God and we have learned enough about His character to know that we can lean upon Him fully.

Some of you have been told that if you will memorise more Bible verses you will have more faith. I have been memorising Scripture ever since I was converted, but if we think that more verses will bring more faith, we are completely on the wrong track.

Faith does not rest upon promises. Faith rests upon *character*. Faith must rest in confidence upon the One who made the promise.

It was written of Abraham that 'he staggered not at the promises of God through unbelief, but waxed strong in faith giving glory to God.' The glory went to God, not to the promise.

So, what is the promise for? A promise is given to me so that I may know intelligently what to claim and what God has planned for me and what God will give me. Those are the promises and they are intelligent directions and they rest upon the character and the ability of the One who made them.

This is a thought that can be illustrated by the writing of our wills before we die. If I should make out my will, I would have to leave my books to someone. I have a little household funiture, but not too much and not too expensive. With the books, that would be about all. But suppose I made out the will and then my heirs come to listen to the reading of this legal instrument. What if the lawyer reads to my heirs, 'I leave to my son Lowell a yacht in the Gulf of Mexico; I leave to my son Stanley an estate of one hundred acres in the state of Florida; I leave to my son Wendell all of the mineral rights that I hold in the state of Nevada.'

You know what would happen, don't you? All of those gathered for the reading of the will would say in sympathy, 'That old man really cracked up before he died. He doesn't own any of those things. He never had a yacht – in fact, he didn't even have a toy sailing boat from the ten cent store. He did not own any of these things, so he actually made a will with no character behind him. No one can make good on that will!'

But, when the richest man in the country dies and they call in the heirs, everyone listens closely for his own name, because this is a will with character and ability and resources behind it. He makes the will in order that his heirs may have instructions as to what they can claim. But if I am a penniless man, I cannot promise and will that which I do not have.

So, you see, brethren, faith does not rest merely on promises, but goes back to the character of the one who is making the promise.

Thus, when I read my Bible, I am given a promise: 'This is the confidence we have in him, that if we ask anything according to his will, he heareth us.' If He heareth us, we have the petition – that is a promise from God. Jesus said, 'Whatsoever ye shall ask in my name, I will give it.' That is a promise from God.

Just how good are these promises? As good as the character of the One who made them. How good is that? Ah, this is the confidence we have. Faith says, 'God is God!' He is a holy God who cannot lie, the God who is infinitely rich and can make good on all of His promises! He is the God who is infinitely honest – He has never cheated anyone! He is the God who is infinitely true. Just as good and true as God is – that's how good His promise is.

Well, where do we make our mistake, then? What happens to our confidence?

We push the living God into a corner, we use Him as an escape from hell, we use Him to help us when the baby is sick – and then we go on our own way! Then we try to pump up faith by reading more promises in the Bible. But it will not work – I tell you that it will not work! We must be concerned with the person and the character of God, not the promises. Through promises we learn what God has willed to us, we learn what we may claim as our heritage, we learn how we should pray – but faith itself must rest down upon the character of God.

Is this difficult to see, my friends? Why are we not stressing this among our evangelical people? Why should we be afraid to declare that people in our church circles must come to know God Himself? Why don't we tell them that they must get beyond the point of making God a lifeboat for their rescue, or a ladder to get them out of a burning building? How can we help our people get over the idea that God exists just to help run their businesses or fly their aeroplanes?

God is not just like a railway porter, who serves you and carries your suitcase. God is God. He made heaven and earth, and holds the world in His hand, and measures the dust of the earth in the balance, and spreads the sky out like a mantle. He is the great God Almighty – He is not your servant! He is your Father, and you are His child. He sitteth in heaven, and you are on the earth.

When I think of the angels who veil their faces before the God who cannot lie, I wonder why every preacher in America doesn't begin preaching about God – and nothing else. What would happen if every preacher just preached about the person and character of God for an entire year – who He is, His attributes, His perfection, His being, the kind of a God He is and why we love Him and why we should trust Him? I tell you that God would soon fill the whole horizon, the entire world. Faith would spring up like grass by the water courses. Then let a man get up and preach the promise and the whole congregation would join in chorus: 'We can claim the promise – look who made it!'

Well, this is the confidence, brethren, this is the bold-

ness. Confidence may be slow in coming because we have
been born and raised in a world and environment of lies.
David said in his haste, 'All men are liars,' but I have
never read that he changed his mind when he cooled off,
because everyone has a deceitful heart, desperately
wicked by nature, and we are brought up in a world where
lying is a fine art. Turn on the broadcasts, and you will
hardly find an advertising programme where the
announcer can talk for twenty seconds without lying. We
have become used to lies on the radio. They lie on the
billboards. They lie in the magazines. This kind of deceit
is all around us, and we pick up that psychology without
realising it. We have the psychology of mistrust, we lose
our confidence in people.

If a man came to my door, a complete stranger, and
said, 'Pardon me, I am here to give you a hundred dollars
as an upstanding citizen in the neighbourhood,' I wouldn't
take it; I would know there would be a catch in it somewhere. We have come to expect the deceit and the 'racket'
and the ruse in everything around us. A young fellow
recently came along and said, 'Good morning, Mr Tozer!'
That didn't surprise me; he could easily get my name from
the neighbour next door. He had a smile that you couldn't
rub off, and I said, 'What are you doing – selling magazines?' 'Selling magazines? I should say not!' he replied,
and acted as though I had wounded him deeply with my
distrust. But after about fifteen minutes of conversation,
he admitted that it would help him through college if I
could become interested in a magazine that he just
happened to be able to furnish by subscription. But he
had a different name for it.

For the most part, we live in a land of lies and deception
and there is a psychology of deceit and mistrust ground
into us from our birth. But when we enter into the realm
of the kingdom of God and the realm of faith, we find
everything is changed – everything is different in this new

realm. Falsehoods and deceits are not known in heaven. Never in the blessed kingdom of God has anyone deceived another. The dear old Bible itself is a book of absolute honesty.

When Jesus was here upon the earth and walked among men, He used no fancy evangelistic manoeuvers. He never said: 'Now raise your hand; now put it down!' We have all heard about people who are supposed to be in Christian work, and wonder if some of them are not scoundrels. Thank God, in the true kingdom of God there will be no dirty cheats who will take advantage of motherly old ladies. 'You remind me of my own praying mother,' is the approach. 'Will you pray with me? I need five hundred dollars to serve God!' He knows she has the five hundred dollars, and so, they pray tenderly, and before he leaves, she writes out the cheque for five hundred dollars, and he is on his way.

I have to tell you that I have more respect for the man who robs with a gun – he knows there may be a policeman around the corner. He at least has to get his money the hard, tough way. But I have more respect for him who takes it at the danger of his own life than for the cheating scoundrel who will take advantage of an unsuspecting person with his soft soap and his hypocritical prayer.

I say this because I feel it so strongly—even if I am considered a cynic and a pessimist and a harsh judge for daring to say it. When I see these things I will say it – even if it cuts my audience down to the song-leader and the janitor and my wife!

Why should I say it? Because, if there is any place in the whole world where we ought to be honest, it is in the church of God. I expect to live and preach so that you can bring people here and assure them that they can believe what they hear from this pulpit. You may tell them, 'The old boy may be wrong sometimes – but he is honest!' As long as I have anything to say about it, any man who is a cheat will never have an invitation to put his feet down on the rug behind this pulpit!

Well, I repeat, the Bible always tells us the truth. God tells the whole story about men. He tells us what we would have covered up.

The Bible tells us of David, a man after God's own heart, and tells us how David fell, committing adultery. We would have left that chapter out, but God put it in. The Bible tells us all about Peter, an apostle of the Lord. But he cursed and swore, and said about Jesus: 'I never knew him!' It tells us that the apostle Paul, a man full of the Holy Ghost, turned on the high priest and said, 'Thou whited wall!' When those around him said, 'That's the high priest, you know,' Paul said, 'No, I did not know, and I am sorry, for it is written: Thou shalt not speak evil of the ruler of thy people.' So, he apologised, and said, in effect, 'I was sanctified up to that moment, but I spoke harshly and I am sorry.' The Bible records it all, and tells all of the past.

So, we lean on the Bible and its truth and its assurance in the things of God. You can trust it – but don't abuse it and misuse it.

The Bible doesn't tell you that if you will accept Christ you will have peace of mind. It doesn't tell you that because you are a Christian you are going to relax and go to bed and sleep twelve hours. It doesn't tell you that you are going to become successful suddenly, and that you will grow hair on your bald spot.

It does tell you that you will have eternal life now, with plenty of hardship and trouble and thorns and cross-bearing, and with glory in the world to come and eternity with God. It makes it plain that if you are man enough to put up with the thorns and the crosses and the hardships and the hostility, you can have the crown – but you buy the crown by bloodshed and tears!

That is what the Bible tells us. It is the good, honest old

Bible, honest and trustworthy. No wonder the saints of God die with the Bible at their side!

Now, what about this record, this truth, this statement of our Lord, 'Ask anything in my name!'?

It means, 'Ask according to His will.' This is where the promises come in – you must know the promises to know that which is His will. Memorise the Word of God, let it become a part of your being, so that you can fully know and count upon the merits of Jesus.

Oh, they are enough, my brethren! The *merits* of Jesus! We are going to heaven on the merits of another – there is no question about that. We will get in because another went out on our behalf. We will live because another died. We will be with God because another was rejected from the presence of God in the terror of the crucifixion. We go to heaven on the merits of another.

So you see, our faith does rest upon the character of God and the merits of the Son of God. You do not have anything you can bring – only your poor, miserable soul. Let me remind you that the bad man who thinks he is good is shut out of God's kingdom for ever, but the man who knows he is the chief of sinners and an unworthy servant comes in humility depending upon the merits of another who is able to cleanse and save him.

If you pray, and say, 'Oh, Lord, I have been a good boy; answer my prayer!' you will never get the prayer answered. But if you will pray in genuine humility, 'Oh, God, for Jesus' sake, do it!' you will get your prayer answered.

You cannot come to Him with bargaining and with promises, but if you will throw yourself recklessly upon God, trust His character, trust the merits of His Son, you will have the petition you have asked of Him.

We have this confidence of God, and we have this respect for His will. We do not expect Him to perform miracles for us so we can write tracts about it. We believe in God but we will never be caught asking God to send us that kind of a toy to play around with.

But you may have your troubles, and you are concerned, and you are willing to be honest with God. You can have confidence in Him, you can go to Him in the merits of His Son, claiming His promises, and He will not let you down. God will help you and you will find the way of deliverance in your troubles.

The grace of God revealed in our lives is a humbling thing; where would we be now, what would we be now, without the promises of God, the merits of Jesus' blood, and the character of the living God? This all adds up to the ground of our hope; not our goodness, not what we could promise to do or be, not what we have done, but the merits of the living God who cannot lie!

God will move heaven and earth for the trusting soul. God will make the river run backwards. God will make the iron swim. God will help His children if they will trust Him – with confidence and with boldness!

# 4

# True Disciples of Christ

John 8:31  *Then said Jesus to those Jews which believed on him, If ye continue in my word, then are ye my disciples indeed...*

Are you some 'other' kind of a disciple, rather than a 'disciple indeed'?

Notice what our Lord said to those Jews who believed and who had begun to follow Him: '... Disciples indeed' – indeed disciples! 'If you continue in my word, then you are disciples in more than name; you are disciples really, and in fact!'

There must be 'other' kinds of disciples or He would never have said this. You see, you can learn a great deal from that which is not actually written. For this reason, everyone knows how one word will imply another. If I say 'up', I imply 'down.' If I say 'long', I imply 'short,' or I would not have had to say 'long'. If I say 'good', there must be a 'bad', or there would be nothing to compare. So, when Jesus said, 'Ye are my disciples indeed,' there must have been some other kind, as well, or He would not have used the expression.

Before we consider some of the other kinds of disciples, as compared to true disciples, notice the framework of

Jesus' discussion with the Pharisees.

First, they had asked the question: 'Where is Thy Father?'

Jesus dared to say to them: 'Ye neither know me, nor my Father: if ye had known me, ye should have known my Father, also.' Then, He continued, 'I go my way, and ye shall seek me, and shall die in your sins.'

Next, they asked the impudent question: 'Who are You?' Jesus replied, in answer, 'I am the One that I have been telling you I am. I said, "Destroy this temple, and in three days I will raise it up again" – and that's who I am. I said, "The Son of Man is in heaven" and I referred to Myself, and that's who I am. And I said, "I that speak to you am the Christ" – that's who I am. I said, "The Son gives light to whom He will" – that's who I am. I said, "I am that bread of life which came down from above to give life unto the world" – and that's who I am. And I said, "I am the Light of the world, and he that follows me shall not walk in darkness" – and that's who I am. I speak and I judge and the Father is with me because I do always what pleases the Father. And I speak from the Father – and that's who I am!'

Please don't fail to notice that Jesus could and did say: 'I speak and I judge – and I speak from the Father.' Jesus was not in the business of offering human advice which you could take or leave according to the way you felt about it. Instead, He always spoke with absolute and final authority. This was not just a man speaking. This was God speaking. This was not just the case of advice from a good, religious man; this was God speaking.

This, then, was what Jesus told His questioners: 'I speak from the Father, and the things that I saw and heard, I tell you. You can trust me, because I came down from above and I represent the Father, and speak from Him, so that what He says has absolute authority – absolute and final authority from which there is no appeal.'

This is quite different from the things we hear about in ecclesiastical circles. Some bishop says, 'It is to be like this...,' but you can always appeal to the archbishop. Then, if you don't like what he says, you can appeal clear up to the top.

But when the Lord Jesus Christ has spoken there is no appeal. It is either Jesus or everlasting night. It is either listen to what He says or be for ever in ignorance. It is either take His light, or be for ever in darkness.

Immediately someone says: 'What arrogance! What intolerance! I don't believe in Christians being intolerant!' Well, I can startle you right here. I believe in Christian charity, but I don't believe in Christian tolerance at all!

I think that the man who hates the name of Jesus, and who believes that He was not the Son of God, but an imposter, deserves charity on our part. I think if I lived next door to him, I would not put a fence between, and I think that if I worked with him, I would not refuse to be his friend. I believe in Christian charity, but I do not believe in the weak tolerance that we hear preached so often now – the idea that Jesus must tolerate everybody and that the Christian must tolerate every kind of doctrine. I do not believe it for one minute, for there are not ten 'rights'; there is only one 'right'. There is only one Jesus and only one God and only one Bible.

When we become so tolerant that we lead people into mental fog and spiritual darkness, we are not acting like Christians; we are acting like cowards!

We cannot do better than to remember that when Jesus Christ has spoken, that's it!

He could speak in truth: 'I am the One who came from the heart of the Father. I am the Eternal Word which was in the beginning with God, and which was and is God, and that's who I am.' This position makes it very plain: it is not Jesus, plus a lot of other philosophies. It is Jesus only. He is enough.

We who are evangelicals and conservative in theology
are often accused of being 'bigoted'. I can only reply that
science and philosophy are more arrogant and bigoted
than religion could ever possibly be. I have never taken
my Bible and gone into the laboratory and tried to tell the
scientist how to conduct his experiments, and I would
thank him if he doesn't bring his test tube into the holy
place and try to tell me how to conduct mine. The scientist
has nothing that he can tell me about Jesus Christ, our
Lord. There is nothing that he can add, and I do not need
to appeal to him. I have studied Plato and the other
philosophers since I was knee high to a rubber worker (for
that's where I came from; the rubber shops of Akron,
Ohio). But I have never found that Plato added anything
finally to what Jesus Christ said. Studying the philosophers
may clarify my thinking and broaden my outlook, but it is
not necessary to my salvation.

I can only say, let us be tolerant of everything that we
can, and let us be charitable toward all that we cannot
tolerate, but let us not imagine for a minute that we are
called upon to take a middle-of-the-road stand, never
knowing exactly what we believe.

An honest heart may come to Him, seeking and yet not
understanding. It may take a week, or a month, a year or
ten years, to help him prove and to help him understand.
But of this he can be sure: our Lord will never, never say
anything but what He has said. Never will He qualify.
Never will He put in a footnote, to say, 'I didn't quite
mean it like that.' He said what He meant. He meant what
He said. He is the Eternal Word, and we must listen to
Him if our discipleship is to be genuine and consistent.

We ought to think with joy about those who are true
disciples of Jesus Christ.

A true disciple has not taken an impulsive leap in the
dark. He is one who has become a Christian after deep
thought and proper consideration. He has allowed the

Word of God to search his heart. He has felt the sense of his own sin and his need to be released from it. He has come to believe that Jesus Christ is the only person who can release him from his guilt, and he has committed himself without equivocation or reservation to Jesus Christ as his Saviour.

A true disciple does not consider his Christianity a part-time commitment, so he has become a Christian in all departments of his life. He has reached the point in his Christian experience where there is no turning back. Follow him for twenty-four hours of the day and night and you will find that you can count on his faithfulness to Christ and his joyful abiding in the Word of God.

Now, what about the 'other' kinds of disciples?

I think first we must consider the person who becomes a disciple of Christ on impulse. This is likely to be the person who came in on a wave of enthusiasm, and I am a little bit suspicious of anyone who is too easily converted. I have a feeling that if he can be easily converted to Christ, he may very easily be flipped back the other way. I am afraid of the man who just yields, who has no sales resistance at all.

I like the sinner who means business, even though at first he will be standing up, looking you right in the eye, and saying, 'I don't believe it and I won't do it!' The time will come when he will think better of it, and he will give himself time to cool off. He will meditate and he will listen to the Word. He will give it serious thought, and slowly but surely, he will make up his mind that the way of Christ is the way he must take. When he becomes a Christian, you've got somebody.

But the man who is a 'flip-flopper', easy to push around, will be easily pushed out again. If you can reason him into the kingdom, you can scare him out again in no time.

Some have become disciples because they found themselves in just the right set-up and in the right frame of mind. Maybe his mother had died the year before, and when they sang 'Tell Mother I'll Be There' for the invitation, he came forward and wept. It may be that all of the time people thought he was a penitent man, he was only thinking about his mother. Christianity on impulse is not the answer to discipleship. God isn't going to stampede us into the kingdom of God. He is true when He says, 'Now is the day of salvation, now is the accepted time,' but He doesn't want us to be picked out of the shell.

Actually, I go along with the man who is thoughtful enough about this decision to say truthfully: 'I want a day to think this over. I want a week to read the Bible and to meditate on what this decision means.'

I have never considered it a very great compliment to the Christian church that we can get up enthusiasm on such short notice. You know, a small tea kettle gets hot more quickly than a big one – but it also cools off a lot faster. The less there is in the kettle, the quicker the steam will begin to fly. So, there are some who get converted on enthusiasm and backslide on principle!

Then, I have met the kind of disciples who seemed to be Christians because of the cult of personality. They had been overwhelmed and charmed by a big dose of winsome personality. You cannot deny that when some people flash their big smiles, their faces just seem to melt up like a chocolate drop, and you want to follow them immediately.

I have always been bothered a little by personality tests, and even though I am addicted to them, I have never found one that really benefited me. But I never pass one up if it says: 'Are you a good husband, or a good father, or have you got personality?' I always seem to come out with a poor score. I once said to Dr H. M. Shuman, long-time president of The Christian and Missionary Alliance and a very wise old Christian philosopher: 'Dr Shuman, nobody will follow me. I can't help but notice all of the big leaders with their charm and personality to spare – all they have to do is whistle, and there come the crowds!' Dr Shuman said, 'Just thank God that they are not following you. If they won't follow you, just preach Jesus, and they will follow Him!'

When you think about it, we are told that Jesus Himself had no beauty that we should desire Him. He was not a personality boy. I think He must have been just a plain-looking Jew, for Judas had to kiss Him to tell which one He was. If Jesus had been a television personality and had looked the part, no one would have had to go up and spot Him. They had to spot Him to know who He was among the other Jews. That's why I think Jesus was a plain-looking man, but when He opened His mouth, glory came out, and men and women either rejected the glory, or they followed the glory. But in any case, they knew it was glory, and they knew they could never be the same again.

Now, let's think about those who are demi-disciples – that is, part disciples, half disciples. These are men and women who bring their lives partially under the control of Christ, but they leave whole areas out, that are not under His control. I came to the conclusion long ago that if Jesus Christ is not controlling all of me, the chances are very good that He is not controlling any of me.

It may sound strange, but I have met Christian disciples who were half saved. Please don't ask me to identify them theologically; I can't do it, I don't know. I am just glad that God is not asking me to please write some letters of recommendation for some people He can't place. He is not asking me that, for He knows where everyone is – in or out of the kingdom – and I don't. I only know this about some of these people whom I see as half disciples: they will allow the Lord to bother them on some things, but certainly not on others. They will obey the Lord in certain areas of their lives, but disobey Him willfully in other areas. The result is, I don't know where to put them. I don't know what to do with them, and therefore, I must leave them with God.

But, as for myself, I don't want to be a half disciple. I want my whole life – all of me – under the domination of the Lord Jesus Christ. It was an old English preacher who used to say: 'If Christ cannot be Lord of all, He will not be Lord at all!' Certainly, He wants to be Lord of all of my life. He wants me to be a disciple who will allow Him to rule my entire being.

I know that some people cannot understand unless you break it down, and spell it out with an illustration, so here it is: A young Christian lad starts out with a shining face. He kneels at the prayer meetings and says, 'Lord take me. Lord, use me!' He seems to be an example of a consecrated Christian man. Then that beautiful little girl comes along. She is not a Christian, but she is nice to look at, has a nice personality and a soft voice. The young man gets interested and she starts to lead him away. Well, there is a wedding, and they get their home set up, and soon he is among those who do not show up for prayer meeting. You ask him about it, and he answers, 'Well, she had another plan for me.' Before long, he is part-Christian and part-husband, and not working very hard at either one.

Now, brethren, I don't want to be cruel but I must be honest. Jesus Christ wants to be and must be Lord and He must be head of and Lord of all departments of my life. You cannot have that girlfriend, or that wife, or that home, or that job, all shut up in a little airtight compartment that Jesus can't control. He desires to be in control, and He must be in control of all of your life – or you will not be a disciple indeed!

Others are disciples – but only for the short term! I have met some of them. They always leave a way out. They never burn their bridges behind them. They never reach the point of no return. I believe a Christian is a Christian indeed, a disciple indeed, when he has reached the point of no return.

The people in our churches would not be worrying so much about whether you can, or whether you cannot be lost after you are saved, if they would just come right down to business, and say, 'Lord, I am not going to worry about theological problems. I am going to face it now, and reach the point of no return. I will not be going back.' But there are still short-term disciples who have not yet reached that point. They are part-time, short-term. They are seasonal disciples. They come to church on Easter Sunday, Christmas and special times. They can be very religious in certain seasons.

I don't know if you have ever heard of 'chameleon' disciples? They are the chameleons of the kingdom, and they can change colours with the crowd. There are even some preachers like that, too. They can talk the language of the crowd they happen to be with. If they are with liberals, lo and behold, they begin to sound liberal. If they are with evangelicals, they begin to sound evangelical. They are adaptable, they say. 'I believe in adjustment,' you may hear a good brother say. Brother, I don't think they need adjustment at all; they just need God.

As Christian disciples, I think we are whatever we are wherever we are. Like a diamond. A diamond doesn't adjust; it is always a diamond. And so, a Christian ought always to be a Christian. And he is no Christian if he has to wait for an atmosphere to practise his religion. Now, mark that! A Christian is no Christian if he has to go to church to be blessed. A Christian is no Christian until he is all Christian, until he has reached the point of no return. Not seasonal any more, but regular at all times. Then, the Lord says, he is a disciple indeed. He is following on to know the Lord!

Now, it may be well to look at some of the marks of those who are not truly disciples indeed.

Some of them just have that pious look. In fact, on Sunday morning, they look as pious as a stuffed owl. We have them in our evangelical circles. We have a lot of them in the Alliance, and we have some of them in this church. They can afford to be pious at 10.45 a.m. on Sundays. It is a most convenient hour. You don't have to be religious to get up in time for church at 10.45 a.m. You don't lose out on your Sunday dinner. You don't lose any sleep. It doesn't cost you anything. You get a little fresh air. It doesn't last long. The music is good, most of the time.

So, the fellow who goes to church only once on Sunday leaves himself wide open to the suspicion that he is only a part-time, Sunday morning disciple. He hasn't been here enough to prove that he is any other kind of disciple.

Another mark is this: they haven't given up their other loves. Fenelon said, many years ago: 'Give up thy loves, in order that thou mightest find *the* love. Give up thy lovers, that thou mightest find the great *Lover*. Give up all that thou lovest, in order that thou mightest find the *One* whom thou canst love.' But a lot of these disciples will not do that – they will not give up their other loves. They want to take the world in their left hand and the cross in their right hand, and walk the tightrope between heaven and hell. They hope by the grace of God to make one last final jump, over the portals.

No, I think not, my brethren. I remember old Balaam in the Scriptures. He prayed a plaintive prayer, and on the strength of that prayer, half of the preachers in this country would have preached him straight into heaven. He said, 'Oh, God, let me die the death of the righteous!' But then he went over on the side of the sinner and fought against the righteous in battle. When he died, what kind of death did he die? Did he die the death of the righteous? I say, 'No.' He died the death of the sinner, because he had lived the life of a sinner. If you want to die the death of the righteous, you are going to have to live the life of the righteous. And, if you want to die a Christian, you must live a Christian. If you want the Advocate above to be a shelter for you in that hour, you must allow Him to be a shelter for you now!

Another mark of that 'other' kind of disciple? Well, he will always be attracted by his own crowd. He will always go to his own company.

In this church, like in most others, there are some who claim to be disciples, who have scarcely attended one prayer meeting during the past year. Dr William Pettengil spelled it out for us some years ago. He was giving an exposition in the book of Acts, and he came to the passage that says: 'Being let go, they went to their own company.' He bore down pretty hard on the fact that even in church circles, we will generally go to our own company. Let some people go, and they will soon be fishing with other fishermen. Let another crowd go, and they will soon be in a music hall, listening to an opera. Let another crowd go, and they will sit in the race park and watch the horses. We will always go to our own company. Christians will always flock together, too. Those that have a prayer meeting heart will be at the prayer meeting. If we have a Christian heart, we will be more than once-a-day Christians.

There are also those who say, 'I am a disciple of Christ,' but they flippantly reject and ignore many of His words and His commandments.

Some teachers have tried to enshroud the person of Jesus in a pink fog of sentimentality, but there is really no excuse for misunderstanding Him. He drew the line as tight as a violin string, and said, 'He that is not for me is against me. He who gathers not with me scatters abroad. He who does not believe that I am the Christ will die in his sins. He that is not born again from above will perish.' In that great day when He judges mankind, He says: 'I will sit on my throne, and before me will be gathered the nations.' That leaves no twilight zone – no in-between.

Consider the benefits promised to the true disciple.

Jesus said, 'Ye shall know the truth.' I think I can help you at this point. No one can know truth except those who obey truth. You think you know truth. A man may think that he knows truth. People memorise Scripture by the yard, but that is not a guarantee of knowing the truth. Truth is not a text. Truth is in the text, but it takes the text plus the Holy Ghost to bring truth to a human soul. You can memorise a text, my brother, but the truth must come from the Holy Ghost through the text. Faith cometh by hearing the Word, but faith is also the gift of God by the Holy Ghost.

Truth must be understood by inward illumination. Then we know the truth. Until that time, we don't. So, Jesus said, 'If you will follow in, if ye continue in my Word, then are ye my disciples indeed, and you shall know the truth.' Continuing in the Word; obedience – this will bring life.

They tell of a boy on one of our mission fields who memorised the entire Sermon on the Mount. He did it in such record time and with such little effort that someone called him in to find out how he had done it. 'Well,' he said, 'I would memorise a verse and then trust God to help me to put it into practice. Then I would memorise the next verse, and say, "Lord, help me to live this one." That boy said that it was not very long until he had memorised the entire Sermon on the Mount in this fashion. I believe he had truth on his side. He did not hold truth to be an objective thing that can be known by putting it inside the head, but objective plus subjective. Then it becomes real to us within our beings by obedience and faith.

Charles G. Finney taught that it was wrong, morally wrong, to teach objective doctrine without a moral application. I have gone to Bible classes and listened to men who were learned in the Word of God, and still have gone away cold as a pickled fish. There was no help, no lift in my spirit, nothing to warm the inside of my heart, because it had been given to me just like a proposition in Euclid or a mathematical formula. And the answer is 'So what? Let's go and have a soda!' Are we aware that we can have people coming Sunday after Sunday as we preach and teach, while we give them objective truth without moral application? If it is true, then we ought to draw a conclusion. It is true; and if it is true, it means me; and if it means me, I ought to obey it. Then you have life. You shall know the truth.

Oh yes, the other benefits. 'The truth shall make you free.' How we want to be free!

You know that passage in Revelation that says: 'Unto him that loved us and washed us from our sins in his own blood.' You know that some translations say: 'loosed us from our sins.'

What does a laundry do with our clothes? Our contact with civilisation makes our clothes dirty, greasy, oily. The dirt is not only on our clothes; soon it is actually in them. You can shake the garment, argue with it, talk to it, and still it is dirty, soiled. Read Shakespeare to it! Or give it a lecture on the advances of civilisation! But it is still dirty. You can wave the flag and talk about our American way of life – but it is still dirty. It must be loosed. Down at the laundry they put the garment into a solution that looses it from the dirt. Then they rinse it and iron it and send it back, clean and shining and starched. It had to get into some solution that could loose it.

The only solution that will loose us from our sins here under God Almighty's broad, blue sky is the blood of Jesus Christ. He loved me and loosed me from my sins in His own blood. Take the sinner and educate him, but you will just educate the dirt in. Refine it – but it is still there. But when Jesus' blood goes over a soul, he is a free man! You shall know the truth. The truth will lead you to the cross, to the Lamb, and to the blood and to the fountain, and you will be free from your sins. But there must be a moral committal. If there is not, there is no understanding.

If there is no understanding, there is no cleansing.

Are you being a true disciple? Are you obeying the truth as it is revealed by the Spirit of God? Are you enjoying the benefits of true freedom in Jesus Christ?

I am just afraid that some of us have carried no cross this year. When we die, we will have no collar sores, no scars on the shoulder that come from carrying the cross. But the true disciple follows His Lord and goes on with Him.

# 5

# Conscience Isolates Every Man

John 8:9–11   *And they which heard it, being convicted by their own conscience, went out one by one, beginning at the eldest, even unto the last: and Jesus was left alone, and the woman standing in the midst. When Jesus had lifted up himself, and saw none but the woman, he said unto her, Woman, where are those thine accusers? hath no man condemned thee? She said, No man, Lord. And Jesus said unto her, Neither do I condemn thee: go, and sin no more.*

It is a foregone conclusion in our generation that a minister of the gospel will have a hard time padding out his popularity in the pulpit by bearing down hard on the subject of the human conscience. What is happening to us in the Christian church, that we no longer believe in the human conscience? I believe that God has given us a faithful witness inside of our own being, and that it is able to single a man out, and reveal his loneliness, the loneliness of a single soul in the universe going on to meet an angry God. That's the terror of the conscience. Why should the church be afraid to admit to conscience, when the Word of God has much to say about it, and reminding us that conscience is always on God's side? It judges conduct in the light of the moral law and, as the Bible says, excuses or accuses.

Not long ago I preached on 'The Conscience' in another

state, and an elderly brother took me aside after the message and told me that he had developed a great burden for me as a minister because of my sermon. Obviously, he didn't believe in the human conscience. Another man, who is in some ways an evangelical 'bigwig', also came to me, and with the same burden – the idea that conscience is to be pushed aside.

Now, I say that hell has done that by propaganda, bringing into disrepute many of life's verities, including the conscience. When conscience is mentioned now in learned circles, it is mentioned only with a smirk. And that's one way the devil has of getting rid of things – get humans to make jokes about them. It is part of the process of the corruption of our minds, for whenever any humour takes holy things for its object, that humour is devilish.

The Light that lights every man that comes into the world is not a joking matter. That power that God has set in the human breast and which can isolate a soul and hang it between heaven and hell, as lonely as if God had created only that single soul – that is not a joking matter. Joke about politics, if you must joke – they are usually funny, anyway – but don't joke about God, and don't joke about conscience, nor death nor life, nor the cross nor prayer. We are fast becoming in our day the greatest bunch of sacrilegious jokesters in the world. It has reached the point where we must defend the whole concept of human conscience if we are to speak of it seriously. That seems almost unbelievable, but it is true.

I cannot ignore that which the universal wisdom of the race has approved – the idea of there being a conscience within the heart of man. I will not ignore that which the universal testimony of all peoples and all ages have confirmed. Neither will I defend that which the Christian Scriptures take for granted in most places, and in some instances clearly teach. If you will go through your Bible concordance, you will find 'conscience' is mentioned in very many places, and the idea which the word 'conscience' embodies is mentioned throughout the Bible; not once, nor ten times, but it underlies the whole structure and is woven into the entire revelation.

Now, I want to tell you what we mean by conscience, as I am able, and then point to this biblical example of its operation, before showing what it has done and is doing to people. By conscience, we mean that which always refers to right and wrong. Conscience never deals with theories. Consciences always deals with right and wrong, and the relation of the individual to that which is right or wrong.

In this connection we notice an interesting fact. The conscience never deals in plurals, but always in the singular. There is only one place in the entire Bible where conscience is used in the plural, and that is where Paul wrote to Christians that he commended himself to their consciences. Everywhere else it is referred to in the singular, and always conscience in the Bible refers to right and wrong. So, it is individual and exclusive. It never permits plurals; it excludes everyone else, and never lets you lean on another. Conscience singles you out as though nobody else existed.

Now, the word 'conscience' in the Scriptures refers to a moral sight – it means to see completely; it means an inward awareness; it means to be secretly aware of. That is the psychological definition for conscience.

But there is also a ground of conscience, and that is what we are concerned with here more than with a psychological definition. That ground of human conscience, I believe, is the secret presence of Christ in the world. Christ is in the world, and His secret presence is the ground of human conscience. It is a moral awareness.

A verse which I quote very often because it is basic in my theology is John 1:9: 'That was the true Light, which lighteth every man that cometh into the world.' That Light has come into the world, which lights every man that comes into the world, is the ground of moral conscience. However it operates, that is its ground. That is why it is here. Because the living, eternal Word is present in the world, present in human society, secretly present, humanity has a secret awareness of moral values.

I know there are some who contend that when the Bible says we are dead in trespasses and sins, it means that we are dead in such a literal sense of the word that we have no moral awareness. But I think that kind of exegesis is so bad and so confused that it should be rejected immediately. It just has no place at all in the Scriptures. It is not true that because the Bible says I am dead in sin I am just a dead lump – that I can't be talked to nor persuaded, nor convicted, nor convinced, nor pleaded with, nor frightened, nor appealed to. They say I am like a dead man until God in His sovereign mercy raises me from the dead, gives me the new birth and regenerates me, and then I am prepared to listen!

That's all wrong, brethren. When the Bible says we are dead in trespasses and sins, it means that we are cut off from the life of God, and that is all that it means. But that, in itself, is so bad that it is impossible to think of anything worse. But that same man that is cut off from the life of God, and so dead in sin, has within him a moral awareness. He has within him a secret inner voice that is always talking to him – the Light that lighteth every man that cometh into the world. It is a singular voice in the bosom of every human being, excusing or else accusing him, as Paul explained it. That is what I mean by conscience.

In this eighth chapter of John we have a biblical example of the operation of the human conscience. Those Jews of Jesus' day were very strict moralists, particularly when others were watching. They were not strict when they could get away with something in private. They found a poor wretched woman, and they had no underlying compassion or concern about her, or about the broken law, or about the spiritual welfare of Israel. They really had only one thing in mind – they were going to deal with this religious teacher who was embarrassing them, and they were going to silence Him for good. They were going to get Him to commit Himself to a statement that they could use against Him, and then, take the hide off Him. They would drive Him out with loss of face, discredited for ever. That was their business and their plot. The woman was merely a pawn, a cat's-paw, nothing more. They had no love for her as a person and they had no hatred of her sin. It was Jesus that they hated, and they would do anything to get at Him.

So, they dragged this poor miserable woman into His presence, and said to Him: 'Here is a harlot, caught in the act. Now the law of Moses says we are to stone her to death. What do you say?' If He said, 'Stone her to death,' and they did so, the Romans would put Jesus in prison and that would be the end of Him. But if He said, 'Let her go,' they could reply, 'We always knew you were against the law of Moses,' and that would be the end of Him as a teacher in Israel. He would be completely discredited before the law.

I must admit here that I have always had considerable personal, private, highly individualistic delight out of the way Jesus handled their approach. He knew all of those men, and He knew their hypocrisy. He knew that they had no love or concern for the woman. He knew that they had no basic concern for the law. He knew that they only hated Him, and He perceived the trap which they had laid. Not only that, He knew their false piety, their phylacteries, their long robes, their sanctimonious look, their affected nasal breathing, and above all, their pseudo-spirituality and artificial godliness.

So they said, 'All right, we are supposed to stone her. What do you say?'

I have wondered if there might not have been a trace of

a knowing twinkle in Jesus' eyes as He looked at those adversaries, and then challenged them individually and as a group when He said: 'Fellows, let the one or the other that has never sinned throw the first rock.' Then, disregarding them, He stooped and wrote something on the ground with His finger. Immediately, being smitten by that inner voice, they sneaked out. One went out, ashamed to say anything to the man next to him, until each one had slipped out quietly by himself, all alone, because it is in the power of conscience to isolate the human soul and take away all of its hopes and helps and encouragements.

Some of those pious old fellows thought that because they were old and had forgotten their early sins that God had forgotten them, but as soon as the voice of Jesus roused them within, they remembered – and they sneaked out. They went out, afraid to look up, perhaps for fear that God would start throwing stones at them, for they knew that they were just as guilty as the woman they had brought into the midst.

That law of Moses that said 'thou shalt stone the wicked woman...' was meant for holy people, not for the wicked. It was never meant that one sinner could put another sinner to death. It was never thus meant, and Jesus knew that. Please pardon the expression, but when these old hypocrites ran into Jesus, brother, it was like a cat running into a mowing machine, so that every one of them came away licking his wounds. Each one was ashamed.

Now, that's how this conscience business works. It smites the inner life, it touches the heart, it isolates and sets us off all by ourselves. To my mind, that is what will put the hell in judgement – that each of us must go alone – alone in the universe before the bar of God. That is exactly what the conscience does; it singles a man out.

So, God has given us a faithful witness within our own beings. I believe that. So John reported that '... being convicted by their own conscience they went out one by one'. Conscience-stricken, smitten inside, struck by a stroke from heaven, they walked out one by one, and sneaked away. That's what conscience does. It is an inner voice, that which talks inside of you. It is one voice that we have all heard.

Some people are still wishing that they could have lived in Jesus' day, so they could have heard His voice and His teaching. They forget that there were thousands who heard Jesus and yet they had no idea what He was talking about. They forget that some of His own disciples had to wait for the Holy Ghost at Pentecost to know what Jesus had been talking about. 'If only I had heard Jesus,' you may have said. Oh no, my brother – you are better off now. You have the Light that lighteth every man; you have the voice of the inner conscience.

Some are sorry that they never heard the voice of Dwight Moody or A. B. Simpson. But I remind you that if we could have the apostle Paul on tape recordings, and let him stand here and preach, he could do no more for you than the Holy Ghost can do with the Book and the human conscience. We have heard a truer voice than Simpson's or Moody's – we have heard a more wonderful voice, the first voice and the last voice. We have heard the voice of the light within the heart, the voice which those accusers of the woman heard. It is sheer hypocrisy to say, 'If I could only have heard the greatest preachers!' Congregations of half-saved Christians will sit and pay no attention to the Light that lighteth every man and meanwhile ignore the voice that sounds within them. The church needs to listen to the inner voice and do something about it!

Oh, brethren, I do not wish to detract from the memories of the great men of the ministry, only to say that they are not the answer to our needs. Don't forget that Paul had his hypocrites, Peter had his Ananias and

Sapphira, Jesus had His very Judas. The history of the great preachers and great evangelists has not been a one hundred per cent history – always there were those with them who heard their voices and yet did not know what they were hearing. You are hearing a more eloquent voice than mine, my brethren; you are hearing tonight a voice that is more serious than that of any preacher you have ever heard.

I once joined a small group attending a noon-day service in New York, and the minister said something which I cannot forget. He said, 'We assume that if a man has heard the gospel, he has been enlightened. But it is a false assumption. Just to have heard a man preach the scripture does not necessarily mean that you have been enlightened.'

No, it is not the voice that enlightens; it is the Holy Ghost, the point of contact. It is the Spirit of God speaking within. It is that which illuminates a man, and makes him accountable to God. The words of a text falling on his human ear may not mean anything; that inner voice means everything! A man has not been illuminated until that inner voice begins to sound within him, and that voice is the voice of conscience, the voice of conviction.

Let us notice, now, what men do to their consciences.

The apostle Paul wrote in 1 Timothy 1:5 that 'the end of the commandment is love out of a pure heart, and of a good conscience and of faith unfeigned, from which some, having swerved, have turned aside unto vain jangling.' There is an emphasis here that some people do have a good conscience, while others have turned away from a good conscience like a stubborn horse. They turned aside, they would not listen to it, and as a result, their religion has become just a vain jangling. They are the Christians who find it possible to live carelessly. But, there is a penalty for careless living, whether we know it or not. Think of these victims who are now vain janglers: they talk just as loudly as ever about religion, but it is merely vain jangling because they have put away a good conscience. All the sermons in the world will be wasted if there is not a good, clear conscience. Such as these are not able to receive and respond to the truth.

Also, in 1 Timothy 4:1 and 2, we are told frankly about certain ones who speak lies and hypocrisy, because their conscience has been seared as with a hot iron. So, there is the conscience that has been turned aside, and here we have the reference to the seared conscience.

Now, I want you to know, brethren, that these who have the seared conscience fall away into false doctrine. We wonder how it is that a man who has been brought up in the Word of truth suddenly can turn away from it into some false religion. You may say, 'His mind got confused.' No, let's be honest about it: false doctrine can have no power upon a good conscience. A false doctrine will fall harmlessly on a good conscience, but when a conscience has been seared, when a man has played with the fire and burned his conscience, seared it and calloused it until he can handle the hot iron of sin without cringing, then there is no longer any safety for that man. He can go off into strange cults, into heresy, into any one of fifty varieties of false religion.

They say that there are now more than 100,000 Buddhists in the state of California alone. Why should there be this upsurge now? I tell you it is because there were at least that many people whose consciences went hard under the preaching of the truth. Then, because their consciences were seared and they could no longer hear the voice of the Spirit, God let them believe a lie that they might be damned. If there are 100,000 Buddhists in California, there must be millions when you take in the rest of the states. Many of these are Americans, not foreigners. Some, of course, may be orientals, but the swamis and yogis that are coming to this country are making converts to Buddha or to their false ideas by the thousands.

Why is it that a man who went to a Sunday school, learned the Ten Commandments, knew the Sermon on the Mount, and could tell the story of Christ's birth and crucifixion and resurrection from the dead, will turn to Buddha or Mohammed? The answer is that he fooled with the inner voice, and would not listen to the sound of the preacher within him. God turned from him and let him go, and with a seared conscience he wandered into the arms of Buddha or the arms of Mohammed.

There are still others, Paul told Titus, who are living with a defiled conscience. You will find it in Titus 1:15 and 16. These are the men and women who are corrupt inwardly, and even their language is soiled. I am just as afraid of people with soiled tongues as I am of those with a communicable disease, for a soiled and filthy tongue is an evidence of a deeper disease that has stilled the conscience.

When our boys were growing up, we were always concerned, like all parents, about the illnesses and diseases of childhood. I remember when one of the boys became ill, I was afraid that it was scarlet fever. I dashed off to the library and hurried to the medical section. I soon read that scarlet fever has one invariable tell-tale symptom – the strawberry tongue! So, I went back home and examined the boy's tongue and found it was not 'strawberry' – and the lad did not have scarlet fever. But I had been frightened. That strawberry tongue is the evidence of the presence of a million destructive microbes within the body.

But when I find the defiled tongue in a human head, it is a symptom of a different kind of disease. I don't care if he has just finished preaching a sermon; I don't care if he has prayed for an hour on his knees – if he can go around the corner to the drug store and use defiled language in his conversations, I am afraid of him! He surely has a disease; his conscience is defiled.

These end up reprobates, the Bible says. I am afraid of

that word reprobate – terribly afraid of it! A reprobate is something that has been washed up, a moral shipwreck. It is something that has been washed up on the beach, and beaten with the sand, baked with the sun, and whipped with the wind until nobody wants it any more. It is no good – a derelict, a reprobate, and I am afraid of it. Let men think of this as they will and explain it as they may, but Paul said: 'I watch my Christian life lest when I have preached to others, I myself should be reprobate.' Yes, Paul said it!

Now, I must mention one more, and I am thankful that it is the sprinkled conscience. The writer in Hebrews 10:19–22 recommends 'a conscience sprinkled from evil works'. Oh, brothers and sisters, I don't think I have the sense toward it right, but one of the most relieving, enriching, wholesome, wondrous things in the wide world is to have that sense of the sudden lifting of the load when the conscience goes free! When God gives freedom to the labouring conscience, the heart suddenly knows itself clean, and the burden lifts, even from the mind. There comes the knowledge that heaven is pleased, that God is smiling and the sins are gone. This, indeed, is one of the most wonderful experiences in all the world – a sprinkled conscience!

A diseased, smarting, protesting evil conscience lays burdened and heavy in its labouring until God sprinkles it and suddenly it goes clean in the blood of the Lamb. Until that time, you can go to a priest and he will give you absolution, but he has only buried your conscience under a little religious rag! If you are ever going to get right with God, they will all come out at you again.

A fellow told me that he confessed his sins many times, and had received absolution, but before he could get converted, God had to forgive them all over again! But when once they are really cleansed and forgiven, you know it, my brethren. There is an inner voice accusing or else excusing. And when once the voice has said, 'Peace!' and you have had the answer of a good conscience, as in 1 Peter 3:20, you can get up and know that everything is all right. No one in the world can make you downhearted then! That is the kind of conversion I believe in; that is the kind of forgiveness I believe in, a transaction within the human spirit.

And that is why I have always protested against picking these chickens out of the shell with a text of Scripture. They sit down with a text of Scripture and pray away till they get a little nose out, then pull him out of his shell, and dry him off, and write down his name as a convert. But you will find those poor little staggery chickens with the 'pip'; somebody picked them out and if you put them all together, they don't have life enough to lay an egg as big as a marble! They have been picked out of the shell. But on the other hand, when the Holy Ghost gets a man out, and he is truly born again, he bounces out into the world healthy and howling. His sins are forgiven, and the load has been lifted.

Now, I close by saying only that it may be fatal to silence the inner voice, the voice of human conscience. Some silence it, for instance, when that voice speaks in outraged protest at the human habit of lying. It may be eloquently pleading against the habit of dishonesty, or taking us to task for our jealousy, or for some other sin. It is always perilous to resist that conscience, to pay no attention to that inner voice. So, I want the Lord to talk to your inner spirit, to your innermost being. Here in our congregation, there is a conscience, that strange conscience that cannot lean on anybody, that cannot share the blame with anybody, that conscience that singles us out and isolates us, and says, 'Thou art the man!' It is the voice that makes us lower our heads and we would like to sneak out, one at a time.

It is here, and I am grateful for it. You see, if there was

not anything like that here or in the world, we would all become beasts in very short order. We would all degenerate morally, and in hell, where that voice is not, and where the conscience no longer exists, it is written, 'He that is filthy, let him be getting filthier still.' That is the Holy Spirit talking to you, that inner preacher that does not preach to a crowd, but only to a single, individual soul.

I am glad that He is here!

# 6

# 'Ye Are of Your Father
the Devil!'

John 8:44, 45   *Ye are of your father the devil, and the lusts
of your father ye will do. He was a murderer from the
beginning, and abode not in the truth, because there is no
truth in him. When he speaketh a lie, he speaketh of his
own; for he is a liar and the father of it. And because I tell
you the truth, ye believe me not.*

We live in a day when it is very hard to find a person who is
genuinely sincere. Most people feel that they are so caught
up in the kind of society in which we live that they must
always be pretending, they must always be putting on 'a
front'. So, they are never their real selves until they get
mad, and when they get very mad, they begin to act
naturally. They let go. I think it is pitiful and rather sad
that about the only time that you can find an American
who is not a 'phony' is when he is mad.

In the context of our Scripture lesson in John 8, there
was no pretending between the parties, there was nothing
that was just being staged for dramatic effect, and the
encounter between Jesus and those who were His declared
enemies had nothing to do with make-believe and enter-
tainment. When Jesus said to the men with whom He was
engaged in a confrontation: 'He that is of God heareth

God's words; Ye, therefore, hear them not, because ye
are not of God!', the atmosphere was that of the battle-
field. When we read this portion, we can almost hear the
whistle of the artillery, the hostility and animosity and
bitterness. We hear the calm but firm, steady and severe
words of Jesus, and we hear the angry, vehement, insult-
ing attacks of those who were His foes. These men were
mad, they were letting go, they had given up pretense.
They were acting naturally, now, showing what they were
within.

So, this was not a showing of theatricals. It was a real
battle and real battles never take place in the playhouses.
This was warfare, and behind it were unseen forces. There
were dark, sinister spirits animating those who had com-
mitted the unpardonable sin opposing the Holy Spirit of
God who was answering through the mouth of Jesus.
Everyone was in deadly earnest – these were spirits in
conflict! Life and death were in this scene – and destiny
and eternity! Heaven and hell were here, reflected in the
force of the words exchanged between Jesus Christ and
these vicious men.

Actually, what our Lord had to say to them was holy,
and it came from a holy heart. It came from a heart that
later was to die for the very persons to whom He was
speaking. Yet, because of the serious nature of their
unbelief, our Lord had to impale them and expose them.
Figuratively, He put them on the end of His spear and
turned them around and let all of the ages see them,
exposing them to the eyes of the critical censors.

There are always some who will argue that Jesus should
have compromised, that He should have tried to 'get
along'. We humans ought to notice something very
wonderful and very different about the Lord Jesus: He was
genuinely what He was, and He was never anything else
but what He was. We presume that He could have 'got
along' with these folks better than He did if He had

wanted to. He didn't have to rub the salt into the wounds, but He did. He did not lose His temper, but He never backed off at all, and He never said anything that He had to take back later.

You will notice that our Lord never had to apologise, for He always said exactly what He meant, and always with exactly the right amount of rebuke or love or compassion. If it had been His ministry to do it, He could have compromised and got on better, but He drew the line sharply, and said, 'Whoever is not for me is against me!' He left no area open as a twilight zone, for in the kingdom of God there will be no darkness and in hell there will be no light. Jesus drew the line sharply between the darkness of hell and the light of heaven; He didn't try to blend them into a compromising twilight.

In our day, the churches are trying to offer such a blend and such a compromise between heaven and hell. Some pastors feel that this is the way to get along with people and to improve the church's public relations. Honestly, our Lord would have flunked any such test on public relations. They wouldn't have given Him a grade of thirty per cent. He would have flunked the whole thing because He was dealing completely in the area of truth, and truth is just truth – it never has to worry about its image. Truth never worries about the effect it will have, about who is going to hate it or who is going to accept it, or what there is to lose and what there is to gain.

Our Lord, was Truth incarnate, and that explains all of the conflict, all of the animosity. Perhaps He could have backed up, and said the same thing in a gentle and half-hearted way, so that there would be no line drawn. In doing that, He would have pleased those who would like to have seen heaven and hell join arms, going down the street in fellowship, saying, 'If we cannot agree, let's not disagree.'

I think it is a different matter when we are concerned

only with opinions, things that are not spiritual and issues that are not moral. If it is only a matter of taste or opinion, the decent thing to do is to say, 'If we don't agree, let's not disagree!' But where there is a matter of spiritual conviction at issue, the man who apologises is a coward. In the case of Jesus and His enemies, they were not dealing with taste or etiquette or charm or art. They were dealing with eternal and spiritual issues, so Jesus rubbed it in, and told them plainly, 'Ye are of your father the devil.' He said, 'You do not know God.' He told them, 'If Abraham was your father, you would act like Abraham.' He took every word they said, turned it around and with calm severity, impaled them. He drove the spear straight through them and held them up and turned them for the ages to see.

Some would still ask, 'Why did Jesus do this?' Well, these people to whom He spoke were moral frauds. On the surface, their profession of religion was airtight. Probably there has never been any group anywhere that held a religious profession that was so airtight. Look at them: Abraham was their father. They could trace their genealogies back to Abraham and Isaac and Jacob. They could go to the temple with pride; they could trace the family tree right down to its source. Those genealogical tablets that meant so much to the Jews were destroyed when Titus took Jerusalem, but up to that time these people could check on the tribes and their ancestry. They knew right where they belonged. Then, of course, they had the temple and the holy place and the scroll of the law. They had the carefully interlocked priestly servants and they all knew they were of God. They knew that; they were able to prove it. Their profession was airtight.

But now the Light of God shines upon them. This Light, that lighteth every man, now shines directly through their careful pretence, through their profession, through their fathers, through their synagogues, through their claims and their covenants.

Jesus frankly and simply faced them with three propositions. Anyone that has ever studied any basic logic will recognise them: major premise, minor premise, and conclusion.

Jesus said to them: 'He that is of God heareth God's words.' Then He reminded them: 'You are rejecting God's words.' That left only one conclusion: 'Therefore, you are not of God.'

The major premise was established because they would have to agree with Him that 'He that is of God heareth God's words'. Then they were faced with the issue that they were in truth rejecting God's words. This is not only sound logic – it is an accurate test of any man or woman in terms of whether or not they are of God. Are they willing to hear the Word of God?

I point out that to hear God's Word, in the biblical sense of the term, rarely if ever means to hear it in the sense that you hear a concert. Thousands of people listen to fine music regularly, but we just listen, we just hear it, don't we? It has no moral effect on us whatsoever. We enjoy listening to good music – but the hearing leaves us neither better nor worse. But that is not what the Bible means. Hearing the Word of God means to hear with sympathy, to heed and to obey. He that is of God hears God's Word with sympathy. He heeds it, gives attention to it, and obeys it. He does what the Word of God commands him to do. If he does not do these things, it is plain that he is not of God. If the men to whom Jesus spoke so severely had been right, if they truly had been of God, they would have heard, they would have been doing right, and they would have kept the truth. But they did not!

That makes it easy for us to lay down and consider an axiom here, namely that we humans 'do what we are'. It is a statement that cannot be refuted. In other words, if a man will let himself go, giving up all outward pretensions, and live just from his desires within, what he really is will come out. Basically, what we are is revealed by what we do, and what we do reveals what we are within.

It is a plain truth, and it is really what our Lord was saying. We should remember, always, that what a man is, is more important than what he does. What he does is only a symptom showing what he is. That which a man does out of desire is what the man really is. That which a man does out of fear will reveal what he is. Whatever a man does out of hate will show you what he is within. What does he do because of jealousy, or appetite, or weakness? That will show you what he is.

Let's consider the matter of man's temper. They are always finding a new strategem to hide and cover that devil – temper! You never read anywhere that a man or woman lost their temper. It is more likely to be: 'He got upset' or 'She was upset.' But it usually means: 'He lost his temper – and got mad!' It is hard for me to think of any man being a bigger fool than the man who flies off the handle and loses his temper. Some of the ladies blame it on their nerves, but more often than not it is a spiritual heart condition and not a nerve condition. Now, when you sit and smile and nod your head when I preach – that is not really you. It is more likely conditioned reflex. When you have a temper upset, that is the real you. That which you do out of your inner being, out of your appetite, out of the explosions of your nature, that is you.

Those human natures were exploding all around Jesus like bombs. Jesus told them: 'All of these explosions of hatred and malice just prove what you are. If you were of God, you would not be doing this. You would be hearing and doing the Word of God. But you are just doing what you are – and what you are doing proves what you are!'

At this point we have to ask: 'If this has been true all through the years, haven't there been attempts to change human nature and human society?' Yes, human society has been trying a lot of things in the efforts to change and do something better with human nature.

We try to do it, for instance, by education. Please don't leave and say that I do not believe in education, for I do. But what I want to say is that education can only domesticate the wild animal. It cannot provide a new nature for a man who is wrong. It may domesticate him. It may condition his reflexes so that he will behave in a pre-determined pattern. That's how they train a seal to perform, you know. Train him to do a certain trick with a fish for a reward, and soon he will associate the word of command with that certain trick and the fish he will get as a reward. That is the way we domesticate animals.

Every oxen knows his owner, but he doesn't come home at night because he loves his master. He comes home because of the association of his stall with his food. The bull out there in the farmyard is a domesticated animal, but once in a while he goes beserk. Unexpectedly, something will make him mad and he will explode and lower his head and roar and bellow. If you are unlucky enough to be in the field, you may have to climb a tree or jump over a bull-proof fence, to keep from getting a long horn through your back. Well, what happened? That bull had simply risen in his anger and thrown off centuries of domestication. He was really the same old wild beast, but he had been educated – that's all. When he got over that spell, he was ashamed of himself, and meekly followed the farmer back to the barnyard. But the farmer does not know when he will do it again, for he is dealing with a bull – tame because of a long process of conditioning. That's all that ever happens when you educate a man.

We read recently of a man who actually had ten years of college and graduate and professional education. But one day he blew up and lost his temper, and the law says that he killed his wife. This is happening everywhere. Don't ever think that it is just the poor and the uneducated and the underprivileged who commit the crimes and the murders; it is happening in all of the top brackets. It takes more than education to change a man's human nature. Education may bring about certain restraints and some degree of control, but just let a man act freely from within, and you will find out what he is.

Society has another way of trying to change people, and that is by law. I am for law, too, as well as for education!

Take the trait of avarice, for example. Avarice means the itchy hand, the love of money, and it is present in most people. If a man is an avaricious man, nothing is going to take that out of him. There is no cleansing water in the Ganges or any other river that will wash away his avaricious, greedy bent. Not all of the soap in the world and all of the fuller's dust can avail to take that fault out of a man.

The lawmakers know that if an avaricious man is turned loose in society, he will break into houses and steal and burgle. So they passed many laws, changing avarice to larceny. In effect, they are saying, 'If you express this avarice – that is larceny.' So the man restrains himself as best as he can, because he has been conditioned by society not to express the avarice that is within him. Often we do not even suspect him, because he has been placed under the restraint of law. But it is still there, nevertheless. He is still an avaricious man. He has avarice in his heart. He hides it and restrains it, because as soon as it comes out and is expressed, it changes colour. It becomes larceny and the law will put him in jail.

We might also take the example of hatred which is found in the human breast. Actually, there is no law against hate when it is within a man's being, for you could never prove your case. It would do no good for our representatives over in Washington to pass a law that a man could be jailed and fined for hating another man. The defendant could be as full of hate as the very devil, but he could stand up there and grin and the jury would exonerate him and say 'Not guilty!'

You cannot ever pass a law that will take hatred out of a man's heart, so what do you do? The lawmakers pass the necessary laws to prevent him from expressing it. If he expresses it, it may be assault and battery, or man-slaughter, or murder. We declare that if a man takes another man's life, he shall be punished. That is to keep the hate within him from coming out. We use education and our laws to damp the fires down a little bit, but the old, ancient fires of Adam are still there in the nature.

Jesus was saying to His foes: 'See that smoke: the old sin-fires are still burning there. You are like trained seals, but you have hatred in your hearts. You have avarice and larceny and murder and you are like the devil. You have murder in your heart and you want to kill me.'

They answered, 'You have a devil. Who wants to kill you?' Jesus said, 'You want to kill me – there is no doubt about that,' and He proved He was right, because they soon did kill Him.

He told them: 'You will do exactly what you are if you are free to do what you want to do. Law puts you under some restraint. Custom puts you under some control – that's education. But what you do proves what you are.'

Deal very much with the human race and you will find that we are the sum of our consenting thoughts. Our Lord Jesus Christ gives us an illustration of that. He was not only a teacher and theologian – He was a great philo-sopher. He knew why things were truth. Jesus did more than simply quote fifty verses, all saying the same thing, like our Bible expositors do. When He quoted a verse, He told why it was like that. That is the only kind of Bible teaching which is valid, in my opinion.

Well, Jesus said to those men, 'Now let me illustrate. He that looketh on a woman to lust after her hath com-mitted adultery already in his own heart,' He told them. Consenting thinking,' He said, in effect, 'that is it. If you think of the act with consent, you have done it, and if you have done it, you have done what you are!' With these words, Jesus explained the incident about the woman taken in adultery.

When He said, 'He that is without sin among you should cast the first stone,' every one of those men looked within himself, and remembered his own consenting thoughts. Each had a look at his own guilt, and one by one they sneaked out. They well knew that there was not one among them that was worthy to throw a rock at that woman. According to the law of Moses, she should have died if they were all holy men, but there was not one there who dared to pick up a stone, and Jesus knew it. They all went away, red-faced and chagrined.

That is an illustration of consenting thinking, and that every man is really that which he secretly admires. If I can learn what you admire, I will know what you are, for every man is what he thinks about when he is free to think about what he will.

Now, there are times when we are forced to think about things that we don't care to think about at all. We all have to think about income tax, but it is not the thing we admire, not the thing we want to do. The law makes us think about that, every year early in April. You will find me humped over that form, but that will not be the real me. It is really the man with the tall hat and the spangled stars there in Washington, who says: 'You can't let it go any longer!' But I assure you that it is not consentingly done! But if you can find what I think about when I am free to think about whatever I will, you will find the real me. That is true of every one of us.

Your baptism and your confirmation and your name on the church roll and the big Bible you carry – these are not the things that are important to God. You can train a chimpanzee to carry a Bible. Every man is the sum of what he secretly admires, what he thinks about, and what he would like to do most if he became free to do what he wanted to do.

How about a lot of businessmen working hard at their jobs? Think of the one who dreams secretly about doing something else, but circumstances force him to stay on that job. His wife has something to say about it. He is on that job but he is really within himself dreaming about what he would do if he were free to do it.

There is no doubt but that a lot of men have been tamed like domestic animals. Many a husband has learned to say, 'Yes, dear. Yes, dear,' but when the wife is not there, you should hear what he says to the goldfish. At times he goes down the street bitter with anger, bitter with hatred, but he hides it at home, because he has been trained by his wife.

But the meekness and the obedience is not really you, my friend. It is what you really think when you are alone – that is you. How you feel about it within – that is you. Oh yes, a man is really whatever his thinking is, whatever his instincts and his impulses are. What he does out of fear or appetite or lust or love or desire – that is the man.

So, education and the law are not enough to transform a man's nature. Many a person has cried out in desperation, 'Isn't there any hope? Isn't there any way to become something else? Isn't there any way that human nature can be changed for the better?'

Some of you who are listening to this are reasoning and considering deep within your own beings. Some of you are ready to admit: 'Mr Tozer, you have been tearing at my heart. I know these things are true. I admit the logic of all this, and I know that I cannot stand clean before God. I know what I have done, I know what I think about, I know about the things I admire most – and it all indicates that I am not good. I ask you, Mr Tozer, is there a way to become something other than what I am? Is the man with hate in his heart doomed to hell where hate must go?'

Yes, thank God, there is hope and there is another way, for Jesus Christ offers help. His Word tells us that we can get a new set of instincts and a new set of desires and a new set of appetites.

The help He promises is not based on your religious conditioning. The Lord Jesus is not speaking of applied religious psychology; He is actually speaking of and promising an entirely new biological deposit. He is promising something entirely new within our human spirit, so that when we do what we want to do we will want to do the right thing. The blessed truth is this: The man who wants to do the right thing and does it because he wants to do it is a good man!

Is there a way to make a good man out of a bad man? Must that bad man sink away into the night, crying out, 'I am not of God. I do not keep God's Word. Is there no hope for me?' He knows he is lost, but must he slink away like Judas and go to his own place?

The Saviour, Jesus Christ, offers the remedy. He says there is hope for the avaricious man. God can take the avarice out and make that man generous to a fault. He says there is hope for the man of high temper. God can cast the devil out of that temper and turn it to a holy direction.

There is hope for you, jealous man! God can take that jealousy out of your nature and give you a zeal for the Most High God. God can give you a whole new set of instincts, a new set of moral desires, a new moral bent so that you will do right because you are right. This is what the Word of God says. This is what the gospel promises. This is the call of Jesus Christ to those who are ready to follow Him, and be His true disciples.

Too often we have reduced the gospel invitation to something like this: 'Put a nickel in the slot, pull the lever down, pick up your prize and go on your way. You do believe on Him? Then take this tract and go on your way and everything is fine!' This may be the beginning of Christianity, brother. It may be the start. It is a beginning, and it is something, but it certainly is not the sum of the gospel.

What does the Bible say about true Christianity? It says that if you will take Christ and follow Christ and do what you should about Christ, your Saviour, letting Him do what He wants with you, He will certainly take the bitterness out and put His love in. He will take the avarice out and put generosity in. He will take the hatred out and put peace in its place. That is what Christianity teaches and promises.

Those enemies of Jesus in his day were perfectly sure that they were right because they believed the right things. They could have joined some of our fundamentalist churches that ask: 'Do you believe the Bible?' and 'Do you believe in inspiration?' They would be taken in for they claimed to believe the right things and they appeared to be relatively right and clean – but there was hatred in their hearts.

So, we are what we do, and if what we do proves us to be wrong, then it is either despair or obtaining the help that we need. Thankfully, no man has to settle for despair, for there is help. Jesus Christ came to help. He came to change our natures. He came to stop old habits of sin. He came to break them and conquer them.

Now, a final word to those of you who can say, 'I have accepted Christ. I believe in the gospel. I believe I am justified by faith. I believe I have peace with God through Jesus Christ, my Lord.' You can say all of those things, but did you ever stop to think that all of that is bookkeeping? It is just religious bookkeeping.

I say, 'I believe that I am justified. Nothing can separate me from God.' That is bookkeeping, brother. How do you know that means you? Has there been any change in your life, your desires, your instincts?

You can claim all of this, but if you are not doing right and living right and being right and thinking right and wanting the right, you are not right! Has there been any change? Is there a great difference since you came to Christ? Do you have that new nature, so that you are a new person, a different man than you once were? You have been doing more than keeping religious books, saying that you believe the right things.

I think we would glorify God by having a testimony meeting right here and now. Some of you should tell us about the change in your lives, you who are new and different men and women, with things different on the inside, your minds running clean and wholesome, no longer in the old channels. Don't let Satan trap you into silence – he doesn't want you to tell of the transformation of your nature. We are going to glorify God now as you witness: 'My encounter with Jesus Christ did this for me. I know I am changed. I know I am different. I know I am a child of God.'

# 7

# Proselytes Just Make
# More Proselytes

John 4:24–26   *God is a Spirit: and they that worship him
must worship him in spirit and in truth. The woman saith
unto him, I know that Messias cometh, which is called
Christ: when he is come, he will tell us all things. Jesus saith
unto her, I that speak unto thee am he.*

We are going to consider what it means to be an effectual
and effective Christian witness as we take a look at the
encounter of our Lord with the Samaritan woman at
Jacob's well.

I am going to begin by saying that there is a great deal of
ineffectual Christian testimony among us today. Much of
it is well-intended, I am sure, and honest and sincere. We
do the best we can with what we have to work with, but
our performance turns out to be something like that of a
salesman selling fountain pens. We try to make a case for
our product but down in the hearts of those we deal with
seems to be a deep knowledge that we are not too much
convinced ourselves. We are unconvincing because we
have not been convinced. We are ineffectual because we
have not yet capitulated to the Lord from glory. It is like
the proselyte making proselytes.

I don't like to confess the fact that, for the most part, Christians seem to be a very sad people. They are not the happy sort that they ought to be, and that is why their testimony is wavering and ineffective. The gleam hás gone out of most Christian eyes and the shine has disappeared from the countenance and the testimony is no longer sparkling and contagious.

Perhaps this is happening because we are trying to plan how everything should happen. Everyone reads a little leather book on 'How To Do Christian Service' and we try to do it the way we have been taught to do it, but it becomes perfunctory and without any contagious element. It seems to me that if angels can weep, they must weep salty tears upon seeing a proselyte who has never really met the Lord making another proselyte who will also never meet the Lord. The woman of Samaria met our Lord at the well, and the Gospel account of that which took place within her soul and the spontaneous, contagious witness that followed, is rich with spiritual lessons for every one of us.

It is interesting to trace in the scriptural account how Jesus quickly drew the woman into a conversation about worship, and how she told Him her belief that when the Messiah came He would tell her everything. Jesus said 'I that speak unto thee am he.' She had come out from the city of Samaria holding her waterpot on her head. She had held a conversation with the strangest man she had ever met – a Jew who had asked her for a drink! – and now she was running back into the city, leaving her waterpot, to spread the word: 'Come, see a man which told me all things that I ever did. Is not this the Christ?'

Let us examine this encounter at the well to find out why our Lord chose to reveal the great and holy secret of His Messiahship to a Samaritan woman. Why was He willing to reveal so much more about Himself in this setting that He did in other encounters during His earthly ministry? He talked about the meaning of His person, His life and His ministry to a woman, and to one who had not been a very good woman, at that.

Why should this be? There were plenty of priests around Jerusalem, with all of the proper credentials dating back to the very order of Aaron. There were many scribes, men appointed to teach and transcribe the copies of the Scriptures. There were lawyers skilled in the Mosaic law. There were religionists in numbers, for Israel was a very religious nation. If you and I had been doing it, we would never have chosen this woman with a shadow lying across her life as the receptacle for a holy secret, a divine revelation above anything that had yet been made, and equal to anything ever made until after Christ's resurrection.

I don't know all of the Saviour's reasons that day at the well. I only know that His revelation of Himself to the Samaritan woman constituted an everlasting rebuke to human self-righteousness. I only know that every smug sister that walks down the street in pride and status ought to be ashamed of herself. I only know that every self-righteous man who looks into his mirror each morning to shave what he believes to be an honest face ought to be ashamed of himself. I only know that priests in their order, rabbis in their proper place and scribes at their tables, lawyers at their work, were passed over, and this woman was given the holy secret. It was the secret of His Messiahship, the secret of the nature of God, and the secret of the true nature of divine worship!

Jesus was able to see a potential in the woman at the well that we could never have sensed. What a gracious thing for us that Jesus Christ never thinks about what we have been; He always thinks about what we are going to be! You and I are slaves to time and space and chronology and records and reputations and publicity and the past – all that we call the case history. Jesus Christ cares absolutely nothing about your moral case history. He forgives it, and starts from there as though you had been born one minute before.

The woman to whom Jesus talked had led the kind of life that made her familiar with the men of Samaria – a great deal more familiar than with the women of Samaria. Yet, our Lord did not shame her and He did not denounce her. Christians have quite a reputation for being among the great denouncers. The odd thing about it is this: they often denounce the ones whom the Lord receives with open arms, and receives the ones that the Lord denounces! That's how some carnal rascal frequently gets into our churches.

That's the danger of proselytes making more proselytes. We need to remember that it is possible to have some kind of an external religious experience that immunises you to the new birth, and puts you where you will never be born again, because you think you are already born again. Because the proselyte never was 'in', he doesn't require the other proselyte to get 'in'. So, it is possible that entire churches are established with the membership comprised only of proselytes, echoes of echoes and reflections of reflections – never the true light shining!

It should be a profitable exercise to think back upon some of the reasons for Jesus' revelation to this woman at the well. There were a number of things that were in her favour.

One was her *conscious need*.

There are some things that do not always follow – they are not always the same and are lacking in uniformity. But there is always uniformity in this area: every person that ever receives anything from God must have a conscious need, a conscious and vital sense of lack. This woman had it. She never fought back, for she was in great need and she was completely frank about it. No doubt she had heard much religious argument in Samaria, and she was a good side-stepper. She did what she could to take the heat off as the Lord's kindly eyes bore into her conscience.

But, when she saw there was no use, she threw up her hands, and was completely frank about her life and problems.

Her frankness, her humility and her enthusiasm appealed to the Lord Jesus Christ as they talked of man's need and the true worship of God by the Spirit of God. Jesus was drawn by her warm enthusiasm and by her frankness and her self-conscious need. So, He revealed Himself, opened His own being to her, giving her the secret that He had not given to anyone else, and that He gave to very few in the days that followed.

When she spoke of the Messiah and His coming, and Jesus said, 'I am He,' the revelation came to her own soul. The light of God slipped down into the shadows of her past, and there within her began to shine. She was lifted in her being, so that she was compelled to run and tell the men.

Jesus accepted the situation, because He accepted her. I cannot see a church board anywhere that would have accepted it. I think the ladies in their aid societies would have raised their eyebrows and made funny little clucking sounds with their tongues. But our Lord accepted the situation because He always begins as though there had not been a past. Behold, He maketh all things new!

We can benefit, too, by noting the *fervency* and the *validity* of her response.

I would not deny that this woman still had a long way to go in her spiritual experience and development. But Jesus indicated God's willingness to use artless testimony and the sincere, candid witness, even though they may be imperfect and limited.

The woman had this one, gracious fact in her favour: she had known a valid encounter with the One called the Messiah. Her heart had come into collision with the revelation of the Person and the Will of God in Christ, and the result was an emotional upheaval in her own life and will.

Now, I confess that I don't know what to do with those Christians and those teachers who are so afraid of the word 'emotion'. Nowadays, we say that a man is very emotional when we really mean that he is a neurotic, that he has lost self-control, that he cries over nothing, laughs over nothing, gets blue over nothing, gets elated over nothing. That man is simply a mental case. We have taken the word 'emotional' and applied it to that. But, I disagree. That is not emotion. That is a mental condition of a man, and he needs prayer and rest.

When I use the word 'emotion' here, I am referring to a person's inner feeling, and I am not afraid nor ashamed to use the word in that way. I really prefer the expression used so often by Jonathan Edwards; he referred to our 'religions affections'. I seem to be so busy that I cannot do everything that I think of doing, but I am wondering why someone doesn't resurrect that expression for our day – 'religious affections'. Jonathan Edwards could show some of these cold, stiff, deep-freeze Christians of the present day that 'religious affections' and the spiritual emotions of the modern day are one and the same thing. There are too many of us who go only on text and theology, and are afraid of emotion.

So, this woman had come through a collision. Her heart had come into vital contact with the heart of Christ, and the result was a spiritual experience which she would never forget. A stroke from God had fallen upon her, and it was little wonder that she started away without her waterpot. Probably she did not know why, but she was bursting inwardly to tell good news that had come to her through the Messiah. It really wasn't much of a story at that time – the Lord knew that, but she didn't. But, it had about it the brightness of a revelation.

Notice this, too, about the sincerity of her story and her actions: they were not imitative, they were not formal and they were not planned, and best of all, they were not programmed!

I really hate that ugly French word as I hate the devil – that word 'programmed'. We have to announce now that the service of worship is 'programmed' so as to have a minimum of preaching and a maximum of enjoyment. But, my point is this: if this woman could have been 'programmed', there would never have been any revival in Samaria, brother! They didn't programme this woman – they couldn't. She had too much bounce in her soul! She was not involved in anything formal – she just ran as fast as her heels would take her. No one planned her testimony for her, and thank God for that! Sometimes we have been encouraged to meet with a group, to 'plan a revival'. You might as well try to meet and plan a lightning stroke as to plan a revival. No one has ever done it yet, and no one will ever really 'plan' or 'programme' a true revival.

The Lord God Almighty makes a world – and nobody 'plans' it. When He raises the dead, no one plans it. And, let me tell you this. When He raises the dead it never comes as the fifth item on 'the programme'. Of that you can be sure!

In our churches, we have fairly well programmed ourselves into deadness and apathy. Think of this woman running to testify with the good news brimming over in her soul. If someone had halted her by taking hold of her garment as she ran, and said: 'Sister, we are glad to see the new light in your face, and we would like to have you third on the programme,' she would have died along with those scribes and Samaritans, and all the rest. But, she went bouncing along, eager to share the new revelation which had come to her heart, to tell the men she knew that she had found the Master, the One who had told her everything she had ever done and known.

That was an exaggeration, of course. But, you know,

brethren, when you get so full of something that you begin
to talk about it, very often your mouth is smaller than
your heart, and exaggeration is the result. I think we call it
'hyperbole' now – that is the learned word for exaggeration.

However, this must be said about her: she was *contagious*. She didn't have to make converts. They 'caught' it
from her by contagion!

Did you ever wonder about the result she produced
with her breathless testimony? The men of Samaria heard
her story, and then started out to find the man about
whom she had spoken. I suppose there was some curiosity
involved, and perhaps an element of the spirit of religious
adventure, but certainly, that was not all. These Samaritans, moved by this woman, went out and found Jesus and
brought Him to the city. They heard Him and they saw
Him and they were convinced and they believed. They
testified, saying, 'Now we know, not because of what you
said, but we have met him ourselves, and we believe that
he is the Christ, the Saviour of the world.'

That which had begun in the shadows had now gone
into the clear sunlight, and the testimony of the woman
whose real life had only just begun brought these men to
God. They found out the truth that you cannot rest on
another person's testimony. You might just as well try to
get fat on what someone else eats as to try to get to heaven
on someone else's religious experience. A testimony itself
does not convert you. This woman's testimony was used
to bring people to Christ, but when they believed in Him,
they said, 'Now we know for ourselves; we don't need
your testimony.' But if they had not actually come to faith
in Christ, they could have started the First Church of the
Samaritans there in the city, based on her testimony, and
without ever having met the Lord for themselves.

So, this is the glory of the Christian witness: it may
serve to excite men and women to get going in the direc-

tion of the One about whom the testimony has been given. A Christian witness is not a spiritual experience for the third person. The witness itself never saved anyone. A Christian witness is an honest confession of what the Lord has done for us, and that may stir others to go and do likewise – to find the same Lord and His salvation.

I must confess that I have never been blessed by a planned testimony service in my whole life. We have had many Christian musical organisations give their concerts and recitals here, and suddenly, a fellow says, 'Now, we will give our testimonies.' Everybody has been told ahead of time who is to talk and what they are to say. So, they all get up and testify and I sit there just as cold as a dill pickle. I just can't find anything within me that responds to that kind of a witness.

But, let me tell about the kind of testimony that really moves me. On a Sunday night about 11:30 pm, my telephone rang. A friendly, lively, excited voice on the other end of the line said, 'Mr Tozer, I had to call you and tell you something that couldn't wait until morning. I have been born again tonight. You know, I have been around your church with my wife, who is a Christian. She prayed for me, even though I thought I was a converted man, but I have never been converted until tonight. After the service tonight, I came into a spiritual experience, and I know now that I am born again!' I knew him as a quiet fellow and didn't know that he could get so excited. He was pouring it on like an evangelist. He has moved from here now, but he is still living his Christian life and praising the Lord. He had a testimony. He could tell what the Lord had done for Him. He had an encounter with God, and was willing to admit that all of his previous religious experience had only been preliminary. Now he knew, and he could say to his wife, 'Mary, now I know for myself!'

But the testimony will start out dead and end up worse than dead if you try to plan a man's spiritual expression and programme his happiness and incorporate his vision. Some people would try to incorporate the glory of God, and take out corporation papers on the divine grace. How low can we get?

Now, let's draw a few conclusions from this account, and apply them to our day.

First, *Christ is still receiving sinners* – even those who are great sinners. No matter what the reputation may be, He receives them all, if they will come to Him.

In Jesus' day, they said with scorn, 'This man receiveth sinners!' They were right – and he lived and died and rose again to prove it, and to prove His right to justify all who come to Him in faith.

One of the old German devotional philosophers took the stand years ago that God loves to forgive big sins more than He does little sins because the bigger the sin, the more glory accrues to the God who forgives. I remember the writer went on to say that not only does God forgive great sins and enjoys doing it, but as soon as He has forgiven them, He forgets them and trusts you just as if you had never sinned. When I first read that, I almost went through the ceiling, because I believed it in my heart – that God not only forgives great sins as quickly as little ones, but once having forgiven them, starts anew right there, and never brings it up again.

We have to be aware of the fact that man's forgiveness of man is not always like God's. When a man makes a mistake and has to be forgiven, the shadow may hang over him, because it is hard for other people to forget. But when God forgives, He begins the new page right there, and when the devil runs up and says, 'What about his past?' God replies: 'What past? There is no past. We started out fresh when he came to Me and was forgiven!'

Now, I think this kind of forgiveness and justification and acceptance and fellowship with God depends upon a man's willingness to keep the top side of his soul open to

God and the light from heaven. You may wonder about such an expression as the 'top side of the soul' but I do think it is in line with Bible teaching and certainly in line with all Christian experience. It is open to God in some people's lives and not in others.

At the risk of stirring some controversy about the implications of election or predestination, I would refer you to the responses of two different men in the Old Testament.

Jacob was a crooked fellow. His very name meant 'supplanter'. He was not a pleasant man, and it would be well to keep your pocketbook buttoned up when he was around. We wouldn't classify him in the natural as being a completely trustworthy man. But for some reason, he kept the top side of his soul open; there was a little window there that was open to God. Esau, his brother, had much more to be said for his character. Everyone will admit that from the record. He was less willful, he was more frank and outgoing, he was more tenderhearted – for he wept on his brother when he should have killed him! In every way, Esau was the finer man by nature. But in Esau, there was no approach through the top side of his soul – no open window there. It was Jacob, the crooked one, who met God and became Israel, because the top side of his soul was open to God.

So it was with the woman of Samaria. She had not lived a very good life. But there was a vulnerable place in her soul, a window toward God that was open, and through which the light of God shone through.

We should know this, also. *New life has to be born within us*, and that new life will not be born until there has been a collision with Christ. A real collision – the sinner has been met and defeated in his own will, his own life brought down to the dust. He will always remember and look back upon that encounter, as happily he goes forward in his faith. His soul and the heart of God met in violent conflict for a moment, but God won, and then the heart of the man surrendered, and he said, 'They will be done.'

Salvation comes to the soul – and this is our need of the day. This kind of spiritual encounter, this kind of meeting of the soul with God, comes as the freshness of a birth, the brightness of a dawning, with the clearness of a revelation.

Oh, let's not be guilty of taking our religion second-hand, of being 'programmed' into our religion.

We have been taught to accept what people tell us, so we do not push on to know Him for ourselves. A person that has to be picked out of the shell, that has to be guided by red lines and blue lines under the Bible verses, urged and pushed and psychologised into the kingdom of God never really gets in. There must be a revelation to the heart. There must be an encounter with Christ. There must be that sudden engaging of the soul with Jesus Christ, the Lord.

If we had our standards higher, if we really preached the truth of genuine repentance, if we raised the Christian levels higher – does this sound like radical religion? Well, it ought to be the normal thing, the ordinary thing. The Lord has told us that power must come to our lives and the presence and the revelation and the knowledge that we believe in Jesus Christ, the Son of God. This is not radical – it is the other thing, the deadness, the lack of power, the uncertainty, that is abnormal.

Thank God for many of you who would stand with me now, and say: 'Yes, I met Him and I know Him. We have had that collision. He won and I lost, and yet, I won, because I am saved! My old will went down and my old boldness and aggressiveness went down. Jesus Christ came in and took over and now, I live no more, but He lives in me!'

Let us come to Him with simplicity, frankness, hunger and conscious need. Come as you are, without one plea, and the Lord Jesus will receive you and forgive you. Thank God that you can go away tonight, saying, 'I have heard this for years, but now I know for myself that Jesus is the Christ, the Son of the living God, the Saviour of the world!'

# 8

# The World Is a
# Moral Wilderness

*John 1:19–23    And this is the record of John, when the
Jews sent priests and Levites from Jerusalem to ask him,
Who art thou? And he confessed, and denied not; but
confessed, I am not the Christ. And they asked him, What
then? Art thou Elias? And he saith, I am not. Art thou that
prophet? And he answered, No. Then said they unto him,
Who art thou? that we may give an answer to them that sent
us. What sayest thou of thyself? He said, I am the voice of
one crying in the wilderness, Make straight the way of the
Lord, as said the prophet Esaias.*

I beg a hearing for the man sent from God whose name
was John, for what he said about himself and about Jesus
Christ is of vital and lasting importance.

If we claim to be students of the prophetic scriptures,
we should take note of how John the Baptist answered
those who came to check his testimony against their little
list of expected ones in God's order of things.

They said to John: 'You have exhausted our list if you
are not the Christ, and not Elijah, and not that other
prophet who is to come. We don't have any reservation
for you. Where do you fit in?' John then plainly told them:
'I am one foretold in your own scriptures, but you have
mislaid my card. You didn't locate me right, and so you
have not recognised me!'

Now, I do not want to distract from the main flow of what I have to say, but I must stop to ask these questions about our own careful teaching of Bible prophecy: I wonder how many cards we have mislaid. How far have we missed God's plan? How many events may take place for which we haven't any reservation, and for which there has been no place in our thinking and praying?

John's answer to their questions completely exhausted their list of expected ones. They could have put all that down on a chart, and drawn crayon pictures of these three expected ones, and then, lowering their voices to a solemn tone, proclaim that that was God's last word on the subject.

It seems plain enough that John did not beat around the bush in dealing with these teachers. He said, 'I am plainly foretold in your scriptures. Isaiah foretold and you have overlooked it. I don't fit into your plans because you want to be let alone.

'You want a dramatic prophet to come,' he continued. 'You want the fiery Elijah to come. Of course, you want the Christ to come, the king of Israel. But, you have given no place in your expectation for one who will come and disturb you morally. You want to be let alone. You want God to conform to your religious pattern. You are perfectly willing to go along with God as long as God will be good and conform to your pattern. It has taken centuries to work out the pattern, and you have a long tradition behind you, and you would not appreciate it if God should upset your pattern or destroy your tradition or do something which is not on your agenda.'

Remember that when John came preaching in the wilderness, he attracted a wide following, because there had been no prophet with the voice of God in Israel for four hundred years. There had been only these uninspired teachers. There had been no strange voice, no inspiration, only the passing along of the doctrines of the Word by teachers telling what others had seen and heard. They were the custodians of theology, and while they faithfully declared what others had heard from God, they themselves had neither seen nor heard.

This generation of teachers was disturbed when John came. As custodians of orthodoxy they were disturbed by the appearance of a man who did not fit into their pattern. When they sent to inquire whether he was one of the expected ones, we discover very easily the extent of their eschatological background.

If anything as sad as this could be amusing, it is almost amusing to consider how quickly the custodians of prophetic truth exhausted their list of expected ones. They said 'Are you the Christ?' and John's answer was quick and blunt: 'No.' They said, 'Well, then, are you Elijah?' and again he said, 'I am not.' They asked, 'Then are you that prophet?' and John's answer again was 'No.'

The teachers of that day had come together and agreed, and had written books, under the influence of the custodians of orthodoxy, that there would be a third person who would come, a prophet so outstanding that he could be called 'that prophet'.

So, we consider their perplexity. John the Baptist was getting a great deal of attention. But he is a figure who confesses that the is not the Christ, not the prophet Elijah, and not that other prophet. That's why they told John that he didn't fit in, that they didn't have a reservation for his coming. And that's why John challenged their traditions and their patterns and their desire for the everlasting continuance of the status quo.

'You want God to justify you,' John said. 'You want God to approve you and the narrowness of your vision. You cannot allow a prophet to come or a Voice to be heard that will disturb you. You want to be let alone, but I am come to call you to righteousness. I am the voice of one crying in the wilderness: Prepare ye the way of the Lord.'

Now, let us look at this wilderness, for that is the basis of this message to our hearts.

The word 'wilderness', as John used it here, does not have the same meaning that it had when he was still in the desert and before his showing unto Israel. There, the word desert or wilderness meant an identifiable, discoverable piece of terrain that one could mark on a map. But here, as is very often true in the Bible, after a literal use of a word, there may follow a figurative use of the same word. We can take as an illustration: 'Give me to drink,' said Jesus to the woman at the well. She replied, 'How is it that you ask me?' and then the conversation went from water to water. After they had talked about the literal water in the well, Jesus said, 'Ask of me and I will give you living water.' So, He raised her expectation from the physical water to the spiritual water.

We know of the wilderness in which John grew up, and now we have him saying, 'The voice of one crying in the wilderness.' Obviously, this is a strong figure of speech and its meaning is not confined to the wasteland where he had lived. It refers to the moral condition of Israel, for John was not talking about botany and agriculture; he was talking about morality and religion. So he went from that word 'wilderness' straight into moral and spiritual subjects. The wilderness to which he addressed himself was the moral condition of Israel.

It could conceivably take an entire sermon to mention and explore all of the distressing characteristics of a wilderness. Let us examine a few.

First, there is the noticeable characteristic of *disorder*. Go into a planned and supervised park area and you find order; go into a wilderness and you will find disorder.

Then, there is *waste*, for there are desert areas involved. There are great sections that are rocky and sandy and barren, without grass or growth. You will find confusion in it all. Consider the great deserts, burned over, beaten up, fallow, filled with green briers and all kinds of weeds, with only a scrubby tree here and there – just a confused wilderness.

It is hard to find purpose in the wilderness. You can drive through parts of our own southwestern states and feel this desolation of the wilderness and the desert. I remember seeing a swayback old cow with noticeable ribs standing near the road in New Mexico. I wondered how she lived on the sparse grass and without enough water. There she was – just a poor desiccated skin holding her bones together. I really wonder why God made such a place, but He made it, and it is there. They jest about some desert areas of the west to the effect that when God made the world, He had a big truck load of stuff left over, and said 'Just dump it there!' I have heard that about several sections, and it emphasises the purposelessness and lack of meaning in a true desert area.

Then, there is the *wild* undomesticated quality of the wilderness. Nobody seems to obey any law around there. No one comes when you whistle, nothing lies down and turns over when you speak. They are all wild, so we have confusion and disorder, waste and purposelessness all built into the wilderness. John had all of this in mind; he knew it and knew it well. He said, 'That's what I see in Israel. God sent me to tell you what I see in Israel!'

The seeing John saw this. There are attitudes and ways in our own generation that godly men and women should be able to see. Maybe some of you think that I am just getting old, and there is a crack appearing in the old dome, but I think I know what I am talking about. I think I am seeing something about the times and about the Christian church, and I hope there will be many others who will be 'seeing', and that we will do something about it.

This seeing John sensed and saw what the religious leaders of Israel could not perceive at all. He saw what the faithful custodians of orthodoxy never dreamed was true. They saw themselves in one light, and God saw them in a different way. John saw them the way God saw them, and John and God were right, and the traditionalists were wrong.

So, he raised his voice for God and for truth in that wilderness.

I know it would be worthless to spend time here if we're simply to attack Israel long dead and vex our righteous souls with the conduct of the Pharisees and scribes and Levites who have been filling graves for a great many centuries. But there is a present condition of the wilderness, a condition that parallels that of Israel when our Lord came. It amounts to this: even though we live in the world's most advanced civilisation, we have been betrayed by our teachers, tragically and cruelly betrayed by our teachers!

They told us years ago that the world was getting better, and I hesitate to use that worn-out cliché. But they said, 'Certainly, the world is getting better,' and cited the statistics that man is able to cure rabies and diabetes and other diseases, and able to do so many things that he had never been able to do before.

But one of the fallacies was apparent in their proposition that because man had become a brilliant toy maker, he had also become a good toy maker, and you will understand what I mean when I speak of man's 'toys'. It is true that man has made and developed and invented and discovered all kinds of brilliant new toys. He can reach up into the skies and pull down the jagged lightning and put it in a box or run it along the wires. At first he could only send your voice along the wires, but now he can transmit that jagged lightning along from place to place, around the world and back, without any wires. Man has invented these wonderful, sophisticated toys.

A few generations ago the toys were plain and simple.

A boy would take a wheel and put a spike through it, and split a stick and run the spike through the split stick – and he had a toy. They used to take an old sock that was no longer useful, stuff it with cotton, paint a face on it, and there was a rag doll for the baby. But now, such simplicity is left far behind. We live in a day of startling electronic marvels. Radio has become one of our toys, and with it has come the television screen. We have invented the deep-freeze as a boon to the cook. We have invented nylon and other synthetic fibres. You can even run around now in a suit of glass underwear. I am not being funny – that is true. They can make it out of glass now. I read about Henry Ford once telling someone on his experimental farm in Michigan: 'You know, I am dressed in soya beans from the skin out – every stitch I have on was made out of soya beans!'

So, we are now able to take a soya bean and turn it into a suit of clothes. We are able to take glass which used to shatter when you hit it and can fashion it and wear it. And we make the fancier and costlier gadgets as well. We make supersonic aeroplanes that fly faster than sound with such fantastic noise levels that the windows on the ground crash because of the sonic boom as they rip through the sound barrier. Yes, we are the toy makers of the world, and because of that the teachers have concluded: 'Man must be better – he knows so much more!'

We have overlooked one little thing in our preoccupation with man's strange and wonderful new ability to take the forces of nature and harness them. He has made these modern advances to make life easier: artificial daylight instead of candles, transportation by supersonic plane instead of by ox cart, wireless communications instead of by runner or pony express – we have all of these and many more. But the sad thing is this: humankind was led to believe that along with our advance in scientific subjects and intellectual knowledge we should also have an advance in moral attitudes.

I don't know whether this will prove anything, but I throw it out for what it may say to a sharp mind ready to hear: I wonder if it isn't very strange and significant that two developments came in parallel order. The toy makers' dream came to pass, the invention of all the gadgets and 'things' that now mark what we call modern civilisation. But, parallel with that, at the same time and among the same people, like two rails of the same railway track running side by side, there came the most frightful and frightening, incredibly cruel and wicked state of affairs that have been known since the days of Noah.

I refer particularly to two ideologies that have been hatched out of hell within our lifetime, appearing at almost the same time as the industrial progress that has given us our technology. I refer to Naziism and Communism. Along with these two godless political dreams there came an utter disregard for human life, with the provision that nothing and no one is sacred except the members of the 'party'.

So there were the gas chambers and pogroms and massacres and purges and starvation and concentration camps and brutalities and murders and death marches – and these have taken place in the same areas where much of our scientific thought was nurtured. Thus, our new technological discoveries, instead of making us better, have brought us to a time of moral disintegration.

Now, I don't want to be quoted as saying that it is science that has made us bad. I only want to be quoted and understood as meaning that science has not made us any better – and something else has made us worse. Attilla the Hun, Ghengis Khan, all of the cruel tyrants of the past – I consider them all 'pikers' compared with these coldly scientific, pre-planned mass murders of our own generation!

And then, lest we take out our sputtering indignation

on Stalin and Hitler, both now comfortably deceased, let me point out to you that the wilderness characteristics have invaded other realms besides those behind the so-called iron curtains.

I would like to discuss the place of women and the degradation of women in our day – but I may as well shut up. There is just no use. No one believes it and to say it is only to have the satisfaction of knowing that you have told the truth, whistled into the wind, and gone to bed! The degradation of womankind in the twentieth century in all parts of the civilised world has been winked at, excused and laughed off. But I must tell you something, brethren: before the judgement bar of God it is not a laughing matter. It is no more a laughing matter than creeping, rotting gangrene in a man's body is a laughing matter. If a man had gangrene in his leg and he could get enough people to glorify it and pay him to exhibit it, and write books and poems about it and sing jive songs about it, he could soon glory gangrene. But that would not change the nature of gangrene – it will still kill its victim just as sure as God lives in His high heaven. Unless the doctors cut that poison out and get all of it, it will kill him. You can never make terms or compromise with gangrene.

The illustration will stand in the spiritual realm: when we violate the laws of God and bring pollution to the purest springs of the race, and continue to compromise in doing it, and then excuse it and justify it, building it into our reasoning and writing books and plays around it and honouring it, we are glorifying something that will kill us in its own time.

I am not sure that we are going to see any change, any repentance, any revulsion against the creeping moral poisons before our Lord comes back again, or before judgement catches up with us. I hope so, but I don't know. And I am not laying all of the blame on the young people of our day and age. I am not here to abuse the youth and their attitudes, for, believe it or not, I was once young myself!

But there are amazing changes taking place all around us, and it seems to me that the rattiest little guy in the whole neighbourhood a few years ago would just be common, run-of-the-mill stuff today. Wouldn't the nastiest little scoundrel with an evil reputation for miles around be just a sort of Sunday school boy today if compared with the average young criminals now taking the play in the worst of the news?

J. Edgar Hoover, the head of the Federal Bureau of Investigation, all the good policemen and law officers throughout the country, those of us in parent-teacher associations and similar groups, are desperately worried because of the changing attitudes now held by segments of our youth. I am not much for statistics, but I should have loaded my gun with statistics at this point. Think of how many crimes are being committed every minute of every day – how many murderers are never caught, the murders that are never solved, the drugs that are coming into wide use, the marriages that have gone to rot. Yet, these are things that we joke about from generation to generation – the same old jokes and cynicism just put into new dress.

Our jokes about marriage have always taken it out on the new brides and on the mother-in-law. I saw a joke printed on the bus ticket in which the bride said to the young husband: 'Honey, I'm so glad you liked your meal. Mother always told me that chicken salad and strawberry shortcake are two things men like best.' And the husband said: 'Yes – which one is this?' Now, I did not tell that because I wanted to joke in the pulpit; I just wanted to demonstrate the fact that the old 'chestnut' is still alive – for there are really only a few jokes. And now they have added another one to the list – the joke about getting married and getting divorced. For instance, the little child in Hollywood says, 'Mama, who is that man that comes in here once a month?' – meaning her father, of course, whom she has never really known.

There has never really been a time in history when people were good, but there was a time when the masses of mankind were ashamed of being evil. We have now degenerated and become demoralised to a point where we make belly-laughing jokes out of our evil ways and our scandalous morals.

Let someone do evil and hide away in the night because of it, and God will say, 'He has gone where he belongs, into the darkness and I will withhold his judgement,' but when the moral philosophy of a whole generation becomes such that men can flaunt their evil and rottenness and wind up with glorification on the front page, then God will withhold His hand no longer! We will rot from within. When we say it is the wilderness, we have our facts before us. The wilderness is all about us.

And if that is all we could see, I would say, 'Thank God for a pure church in the midst of all this night; thank God for a pure woman with the light in the midst of this darkness' – but I cannot say that and tell the truth. For the Christian church, instead of floating high above it all, free and clean and separated, finds her poor old boat leaking water from every seam, and now the church and the world have become so mixed up that it is hard to tell one from the other. The world has so affected our moral standards that Christians say they believe in Christ and yet have never bothered to change their moral attitudes and standards at all.

As in John's day, so it is in ours. The religious leaders were defending themselves and their traditions. They wanted to be let alone and approved. They did not want to be disturbed. They wanted to go to church because 'it is so peaceful there'. They said, 'Oh, it is so peaceful sitting here in church. It makes me feel so good!' They wanted to go to church so they could feel good. But all around them the wilderness conditions prevailed.

The cowardly leaders made converts but it was to the morally purposeless and vain manners of the day. Now, we preach the gospel, we say, and make converts – but we make converts to the wilderness, too! We make converts to the futility, to the emptiness. I don't know that God will raise up another John, but if He should do so before Jesus comes, one of the first things for which we may as well get set, is to be disturbed, deeply disturbed. Perhaps even angered!

Let us look at our situation – at this church alone. Common honesty requires me to say, and God will have to show me if I am wrong, that compared with the average church, this church is a good church. I suppose that a large percentage of our people are good people and moral people, a large percentage could lead in prayer if called upon, a large percentage could lead another soul to Christ. Most of our people give largely to missions and to other good causes. This must be, or we would not have such a large amount coming in to our church year after year.

So, I must say, in defence of the church, that compared to the average fundamentalist group, it must be considered an unusually good church. But, even in this congregation, how much disorder there is! Compared with what we ought to be, brethren, how much disorder there is in our lives – just spiritual disorder in the life and in the heart!

How much waste there is in our lives. There is waste of the vital gifts of God, waste of abilities of life and time. The wilderness is characterised by waste – spaces that have gone to waste and are no good to God or man. Many of you Christians to whom I am preaching now – many would have to say: 'It is true, Mr Tozer, my heart is more like a wilderness than like a garden; more like the stretches beyond Jordan than like the garden of God!'

Very little grows in the wilderness, and nothing matures. If there is any fruit, it is scrubby. If there is any grain, it is inferior because of the barrenness. What do we have to show our Lord for our service? How tragic to have been born again and yet have no fruit to show for our Christian faith – to go our way never having actually done anything for Him.

# 9

# The 'Spiritual-or-Secular' Tightrope

John 6:5–11  *When Jesus then lifted up his eyes, and saw a great company come unto him, he saith unto Philip, Whence shall we buy bread, that these may eat? And this he said to prove him: for he himself knew what he would do. Philip answered him, Two hundred pennyworth of bread is not sufficient for them, that every one of them may take a little. One of his disciples, Andrew, Simon Peter's brother, saith unto him, There is a lad here, which hath five barley loaves, and two small fishes: but what are they among so many? And Jesus said, Make the men sit down. Now there was much grass in the place. So the men sat down, in number about five thousand. And Jesus took the loaves; and when he had given thanks, he distributed to the disciples, and the disciples to them that were set down; and likewise of the fishes as much as they would.*

Before we look at this portion which brings us to a consideration of Philip, a man with a calculator, Andrew, a man with a suggestion, and an unnamed boy willing to surrender his lunch to the Lord, it will be well for us to note the fact that Jesus went into the mountain and just sat with His disciples prior to the miraculous feeding of the multitude.

It seems plain that Jesus withdrew from the great press of the people, and I would like to say to you that there are some things that you will never learn with anyone else present. I believe in church and I love the fellowship of the assembled brethren, and there is much we can learn when we come together on Sundays and sit among the saints; but there are certain things that you will never learn when others are with you.

There is no question but that part of our failure today is religious activity that is not preceded by an aloneness, an inactivity. I mean the art of getting alone with God and waiting in silence and in quietness until we are charged, and then, when we act, our activity really amounts to something, because we have been prepared for it.

Those who practise inactivity among us generally do not practise the kind recommended in the Bible, the kind of quiet waiting our Lord practised. Some of what we see today is just plain laziness, and the Lord hasn't anything good to say about the sluggard. There isn't one lonely text in the sixty-six books of the Bible that says anything kind about the sluggard. So, the inactivity that arises out of sheer laziness has no place in the Bible.

There is also the activity that stems from fear. People who are fearful of doing anything at all figure that they can cut down and narrow the area of their peril by doing nothing. They feel that if they simply stand still, there will be less danger of getting into trouble. God never sanctions this kind of inactivity, for it springs out of our own motive of fearfulness.

Others are inactive because of lack of vision and the confusion that results. People just don't know what to do, so they don't do anything! I think great sections of the church are in that condition. These are people who have never seen a path and they don't know where to find one. They have no highway stretching ahead, so they stand still. They don't know what to do; they lack vision.

But there is an inactivity which, paradoxically, is the highest possible activity. There can be a suspension of the activity of the body as when our Lord told His disciples to tarry until they were filled with the Holy Ghost – and they did! They waited on God.

The Old Testament is full of these expressions of waiting on God. It is good for a man to wait on God. In the Old Testament it meant coming before the presence of the Lord with expectation and waiting there with physical inactivity and mental inactivity. 'Cease thy thinking, troubled Christian...' – a place where the mind quits trying to figure out its own way and throws itself wide open to God, and the shining glory of God comes down into the life and imparts an activity.

I wonder if you understand what I mean when I say that we can go to God with an activity that is 'inactive'. We go to God with a heart that isn't acting in the flesh or in the natural – trying to do something – but going to God and waiting. It just means that within, our inner spirit is seeing and hearing and mounting up on wings, while the outer, physical person is inactive, and even the mind is to some degree suspended.

Now, we know that Jesus once rebuked a woman for being too active – and that was Martha. Sometimes we are prone to add a good deal to what the Lord actually said. I have discovered that the Lord's kindly rebukes to Martha have been a cue for the preachers to abuse the poor woman. I think we abuse her too much and I personally thank God for the Marthas in the world. Someone generally has to cook and do the dishes and see that the work gets done. Without the Marthas in the world, we wouldn't be so sleek and well-fed, and the Lord's rebuke to Martha was enough. I don't think you and I ought to add so many licks to the chastisement that the Lord gave her.

But, notice, on the other hand, that Mary was there,

simply sitting. It is the same word that John uses for the inactivity of Jesus when He went up into the mountain and sat. Mary was simply sitting at the feet of the Saviour, and the Lord rebuked Martha for her nervous activity. I think she just carried her activity beyond the point where it did any good, and she didn't back it up by an inward spiritual relaxation.

Now, in the case of our Lord, the people came to Him, I note here, and He was ready for them. He had been quiet and silent and had sat alone and meditated. Looking upward, He waited until the whole hiatus of divine life moved down from the throne of God into His own soul. He had become poised and like a violin, tuned, and like a battery, charged, was prepared for them when they came.

So these were the people – this great multitude without anything to eat, a great mob that had charged out and followed the Lord. Some brought their babies, and some were old, and some were not strong, and now after three days on the way their food had given out. They were in need, but there was no place where anyone could buy food.

It was then that the Lord said to Philip, 'Whence shall we buy bread?' Does that say anything to you? It says to me that our human Lord was concerned with bread.

There has never been a camp meeting that didn't have a kitchen and dining hall attached. There never has been a pentecost anywhere that didn't have a cook somewhere around the corner to feed the Spirit-filled saints. Our Lord knows that we are human beings – it is good for us to know that He understands everything about us.

I have wondered why God gave us a body and tied us down here, and I have concluded that He gave us these bodies more or less as a discipline. I don't know what else they are for. Emerson wrote at one time that nature had one function toward human beings and that was to discipline them.

We are bound to think like this occasionally for the body gets a little out of hand at times, and we have to spend as much time and energy and care looking after this 'tabernacle' as we do looking after all of the rest of the family, and the daily business, too. But I am glad that God understands about it and He knows. He gave us these mortal frames and He expects us to take care of them, and we see in this setting that He was concerned about the people having something to eat.

I have never believed in the great distinctions that some people try to make between the sacred and the secular, and I believe that eating can be just as religious a thing as praying. I believe that it is just as spiritual to eat my breakfast as it is to have family prayers. Further, I believe that the man who separates his breakfast from his prayers is making an unnecessary division. Why should he put eating in one category and apologise to the Lord saying: 'I'm awfully sorry, Lord, but you know I have to eat now. I'll be seeing you as soon as I am through, but excuse me now while I am busy eating.'

I think it is wrong to place our physical necessities on one side, and put praying and singing and giving and Bible reading and testifying on the other side. How can we say, 'This is spiritual' and 'This is secular'? We actually try to walk a tightrope in between – a kind of a braiding, a lacing in and out – the secular and the spiritual, apologising to God when we must turn aside for a little while to do something 'secular'.

Well, my brother, I have a better way than that for living, and I can tell you that the Lord Jesus never made the distinction that many do. He said He was the Lord. He was God Himself and He said, 'Where will we get bread that these may eat?' When He broke the loaves and passed them along to that great multitude, they ate, and the eating was as spiritual as the teaching had been. The teaching and the eating were equally spiritual, and the praying that preceded the meal was just as spiritual – but no more so – than the eating.

Now, if you can get hold of that, it will mean a wonderful thing to you – that the Lord is the Lord of our bread and the Lord of our eating and the Lord of our bathing and the Lord of our sleeping and Lord of our dressing, and Lord of our working, so that when we work, we need not say, 'Now, Lord, I have to work today so I'll see you tonight.'

Our Lord is with us, sanctifying everything we do, provided it is honest and good. God doesn't sanctify the bartender's activities. No bartender can pray in the morning and say, 'Now, Lord, be with me today,' because God isn't going to work with a bartender. You can tell that I am sure about that, although I am not so sure about the downhill trends, and the rapid changes in churches and religious life. Is it possible that we could ever see the formation of a society of bartenders and beer vendors who will paint John 3:16 on the bottom of those mugs so that when the glass is drained, there is the 'witness' of John 3:16? Would the drinkers say: 'Why, these dear people are Christians! They are good Christian bartenders and beer vendors! Look there, at the text on the ceiling. It says "The Lord is with thee, be not afraid!" They are witnessing with a good Bible text – don't say they are not Christians!' No, I am sure that the Lord is not going to bless the gambler and the bartender. But, if your job is decent and respectable, the Lord is going to bless it, and if the Lord is in you, He will be in your labours.

Well, notice that it was the Lord of Glory that said: 'Whence shall we buy bread that these may eat?' He, Himself, was concerned with our eating; He didn't delegate that concern to a prophet nor to an angel. These hungry people were really Jesus' problem, but He made it Philip's problem; He honoured Philip by taking him in with Him.

I remember that I preached a sermon quite a while ago

in which I said that the Lord is self-sufficient and doesn't really need us. I know I bothered some people by that, for I assume that they thought the Lord really needed them, and if they should retire or resign, the Lord would have to scramble around to try to find someone who could take their place. What a low view of God that is, my brother! Could you get down on your prayer bones and bend your knee and cry to a God that needed you? I couldn't. A God that needed me would be a God in real trouble. He doesn't have to have me, nor you either. That may be bitter for some people to accept, because we have come to believe that we are indispensable, and when we go, a great tree will have fallen, leaving a vacant place against the sky. Brother, I am afraid that when some of us die, it will be like a stalk of grass that was eaten by a grasshopper and nobody noticed the difference!

But, in this passage, here were these hungry people and the Lord was going to feed them. The thing is, He didn't want to just feed them and have it over with. He wanted some blessing to flow all around as a result of it, so He picked out one of His disciples, saying to Himself: 'I am going to take Philip in on this; I am going to honour him by letting him become a part of this plan. He can help Me work it out, although actually I do not need him at all.

So, Jesus encouraged Philip to tackle the problem along with Him. He nudged Philip a little and got him into a hard spot, just to reveal to Philip his own emptiness.

Now, my friends, it is never a waste of time to learn that you don't know every answer and it is never a waste of time to learn how little you have. It is a positive victory for me when I learn things that I cannot do – a positive victory when I learn the things that I haven't got.

Actually, there is so little filling of our vessels these days because there is so very little of emptying. The Lord had to empty Philip in order that He might fill him, for Philip was full of his own ideas. The Lord cannot fill with

His own presence that which is already full of something else and refuses to be emptied. Actually, Philip didn't acquit himself very well here. The Lord said, 'Philip, where are we going to buy bread that these may eat?'

Philip revealed the type of mind that is altogether earthly, uninspired and uninspiring. Here is what Philip did. He reached in and took out his pencil and pressed a button and went to work, and he brought his pencil to bear on the miracle. With his pencil and pad of paper he became Philip the Calculator.

This makes me wonder why we don't name people the way they used to. They used to name people according to what they were. Even in the country places when I was growing up they named people according to what they were. Black Simon Finnegan was a man in our neighbourhood. He wasn't any blacker than I was. He was a white man but his name was Black Simon. Another man was called Little Simon. They distinguished them. If you will look back in history, you will find men with distinguishing names, like Eric the Red and Alexander the Great.

Now, I wonder why we couldn't go to the New Testament and name some of the characters. Here was Philip the Calculator, Philip the Mathematician, Philip the Clerk. There was a need for a miracle and Philip took out his pencil to figure the odds. I guess every Christian group has at least one boy with the pencil. I have sat on boards for a good many years, and there is rarely a board that doesn't have Philip the Calculator present. When you suggest something, he takes out his pencil and leans back a little and leaves a few streaks on the wall and comes up with proof that you can't do it. You can't do it!

Before we built this church, there was an old milk barn here. When we talked about building this church, we had more Philips who said, 'It can't be done!' And of course, they could prove it! Well, we built it anyway, and paid for it in six years. But it was something that just couldn't be done, and the pencil and the pad proved it.

I have been sitting on these boards for many years, and there are always two kinds of men – those who can see the miracle and those who can only see the pad and the pencil. Philip went to work with his pencil. He knew how much money there was among the disciples, and how much a loaf of bread sold for and how many slices you could get out of each loaf, and he knew the size of the hungry crowd. He then turned to the Lord and said, 'Two hundred pennyworth of bread is not sufficient for them that everyone may take a little.' Then he walked away. He had made his contribution, and it was one hundred per cent negative. If they had listened only to Philip, they would have dropped starving in the wilderness. The glorious miracle would never have taken place.

Philip the Calculator, the man with the pencil. He is a dangerous man, brother, in the church of our Lord Jesus Christ. Every suggestion made in the direction of progress is voted down by the church.

Next we come to the other man, and that was Andrew. He did a little better than Philip. He made a timid suggestion, and said, 'There is a lad here and he has a little lunch – five barley loaves and two small fishes.' Then he added, 'But what are these among so many?'

Now, I wouldn't call Andrew a world-beater on the basis of this account, and if he were living now, he wouldn't be what we would call a 'founder' nor a 'promoter' – that's sure enough. Andrew was only partly over on the side of the 'wonder' – only partly. Andrew looked around and said, 'Surely this final tally at the bottom of the column isn't the end of things. My brother Philip is a good boy and I like him, but he is a bit on the negative side.' He looked at all of the figures on that – so much bread for so many pennies, so many people, slice the bread into so many. 'No,' he said, 'it is no use – it will merely be a trifle for each one. But that can't be the end. There must be help, there must be a way.'

So, the man Andrew begins to look around. You will be getting a little closer to the miracle when you can get a church full of Andrews. Even if you have only one or two Andrews, you will usually have a footnote, and one of them will say, 'There is a boy here that has a lunch, some bread and fish, but then, after all, that's not very much...' and there's a rising inflection in the voice which is an invitation for someone to come to his rescue. 'If I can get a little encouraging word from someone, I think I can see some hope in the situation' – that's Andrew.

Personally, I think you are getting a little warmer when you are like Andrew, my brother! Philip was as cold as ice, with his adding machine and his computer proof that nobody was going to eat on that occasion. But Andrew looked around and said, 'Well, we have a start. We have a little lunch here. A little basket. A lad. A boy.'

I must tell you that I have never been able to figure out how that boy managed to hang on to that lunch. Boys that I know would have had it eaten by 9 a.m. the first morning, and here it was the third day. But he was still holding on to the little lunch. Perhaps his good mother had given him a little extra and he still had it. The five loaves were really only slices, not loaves but simply glorified pancakes. That's all they were, with two small fishes.

So, that was the lad. Andrew, himself, had nothing, but he knew someone with a little lunch. That might help out a bit, he thought. I think of Andrew as being a help on any church board, because at least he was looking around for a fellow with a lunch. This speaks of a little note of hopefulness, and a little faith. Those who sit in the board meetings and talk the church down give me a clue about the sheep to whom Jesus referred. All you have to do to begin to kill a church is to begin to talk it down. Just let the sheep begin to bleat the blues and the thing will die in no time at all. Just begin to bleat the blues. The power of suggestion will likely take care of the rest of the downfall.

It can be like that in churches, you know. You can talk a church down and one fellow will meet another and say, 'Things aren't going so well, are they?' 'No, not going so well.' Another fellow will say, 'Not going so well,' and gets the response, 'That's what I have been hearing.' He had just heard it five minutes before from another fellow. So it soon comes out: 'Have you heard what the talk is?' Before long, they have talked that church down, and with the calculators and the buttons, the mathematicians have seen the pencil and the problem, but they have not seen God. They have figured things out but they have not figured God in.

Brethren, it is time that we at least find an Andrew or two, men who have hope and faith to look around for a token. That's all that lunch was – merely a token. It wasn't very much. It really was not enough for more than one. But Christ took that inadequate token and made it enough for more than five thousand persons.

You will remember that I have quoted a little passage I got from dear old Walter Hilton who lived before the time of Shakespeare. He was talking about how we ought to serve God and how much we ought to give and how we ought to go about serving God. He said: 'I will give you a little rule.' Then he used the old English word 'mickle' which meant 'much'. 'Mickle have, mickle do. Let have, let do. Nothing have, at least have a good intention.' If you haven't got mickle or much, then do what you can. If you haven't anything, then have a good intention. I think that's a good rule, and Andrew at least had a good intention and a lunch, a token. He was on God's side, at least far enough.

You may note that it doesn't really tell us how they got that lunch. It says that Jesus took the loaves; it doesn't say how He got them, but I have read too much about my

Lord to believe that there was any force or compulsion involved. That lunch must have been vitally important to that boy, but he surrendered it to Jesus.

Perhaps Jesus smiled and said to the boy, 'Would you like to do something that would help all of these hungry people gathered here?' The happy-faced boy looked up and said, 'Certainly, Master.' 'Well, then, let me have your lunch.' I think the boy grinned and handed it to Jesus, who turned to the disciples, and said, 'All right, tell the people to sit down.'

So, they sat down in orderly rows, in tiers of rows, and Jesus took the bread and blessed it and lifted up His heart and said, 'Oh God, bless this little bit. Bless this little bit of optimistic hope. Bless this token of belief.' And then He began to spread it around, and suddenly there were baskets full. Where did the baskets come from? Those were the lunch baskets from which the people had eaten a day or two before. There had been plenty of empty baskets in that crowd, but only one lunch. Jesus took the one lunch and multiplied it so there was food for all, because it had been surrendered for His use, for the blessing of more than five thousand.

All of this brings us to a question: Are you a Philip? Are you an Andrew? Are you a little lad?

Philip was so good at figures that he forgot to figure God in. Andrew was a little nearer; he didn't have anything but he knew where he could dig up something. And then there was the lad. He didn't have much, either, but what he had he gave to the Lord Jesus, who had the power to make it sufficient.

Which side are you on?

Are you standing with those who are convinced that the Lord cannot do anything – they have everything? They are sure of themselves. They have everything figured out.

Are you among the uncertain ones, whose hearts are on the right side? They are sure that the lunch is not enough, but they are hopeful, because it is something.

Then, some of you are right with the lad, who says: 'If I give you this lunch, Master, it means I don't eat, but I like the way You do things, and I am willing to go along with You. Will You take it?'

Here I should tell you that I think that when the Lord sent a basket of that food to the lad, He put an extra fish on top. I think He did. It is quite in keeping with the ways of the Lord – to put a little extra in the basket of the fellow who had given his all. I know He does this in spiritual things, so why shouldn't He do it with a lunch?

So, I recommended that we ask God for at least the grace of an Andrew – that we begin to look around for tokens of the grace of God – and we will find those tokens. You may have a token, my brethren, and do not know it. Do you think the lad knew that he had the key to the miracle? No, he did not know, but he had it and carried it in his lunch basket. He had lugged it for three days and didn't know it. You may have in your possession the key to the future. You may have in your hand, without knowing it, the key to the salvation of at least ten, and perhaps a hundred, if you only knew it. You need only surrender and let the Lord have it.

Say to Him, now, 'Master, I only have a token, a little token, but take it, Lord Jesus, take it!' The Lord will take it. How He will multiply it I do not know, but He can do it and He will do it.

But He has to have a surrendered lunch – some token that you alone can surrender into His hands.

# 10

# The Church Is on a Stormy Sea

John 6:19–21  *So when they had rowed about five and twenty or thirty furlongs, they see Jesus walking on the sea, and drawing nigh unto the ship: and they were afraid. But he saith unto them, It is I; be not afraid. Then they willingly received him into the ship; and immediately the ship was at the land hither they went.*

I am bringing this message to you as a message of encouragement in a time of political and social and economic upheaval, when the loud and belligerent statements of dictators and rulers who have big mouths, and little tight hearts are the winds that are stirring the sea.

But in the midst of all the turmoil in the earth, there is one walking on the storm and His name is Jesus Christ, the Lord. We ought never to be frightened, not for a moment, because He is the Sovereign Lord.

Now, I think there is a vivid picture in the text, as the frightened disciples invited Jesus into the storm-tossed boat, and immediately they were at the shore!

As you know by this time, I am not what you would call a preacher of Bible types. I think there are a few types in the Old Testament, but I think they have been greatly overdone and over-emphasised. I think that we have been bound by a slavish conformity to types which were created for us by Bible expositors who would have saved us a great deal of trouble if they had been knitting at the time, instead of teaching.

But there is more than a story here. It is a divine drama. It is God Almighty moving in audacity through the universe on His way to His predestined end, and it was not by chance or accident that our Lord went up into the mountain and the disciples went down to the sea. I do not claim to exhaust the meaning, for there is an infinite variety of helps which the soul can gather from this recorded event. But I believe the Lord was giving us a very beautiful object lesson, and it will lead us into thoughts concerning the hope of His return to the earth.

Now, there is something else that I wish to say right here. You don't have to be technical and dogmatic and unbending about the Second Coming of Christ. Frankly, I think we have spoiled the hope of Christ's coming by a lot of unyielding charts and lines and circles in our prophetic teaching during the first half of the twentieth century. Some of our sensational prophets have been wiser than Isaiah, and they have quoted more Scripture than Daniel, and because of their meticulous and detailed plans of the Second Coming in prophecy, they have frightened many away from a vital belief and hope in the imminent return of Christ to this earth.

But they haven't frightened me away, brethren. I believe it with all of my heart. That Bible teacher with his chart and his red pencil can offer me his details and I will smile and wait patiently for the coming of the Lord. I believe that He is going to walk down on our troubled sea, and He is waiting for the church to invite Him in. Perhaps we don't need Him badly enough, brethren. When our need here is so great that we can no longer get along without Him, He will come!

Now, there are some beautiful and inspiring things we

should note about the Person of the Lord Jesus Christ as we proceed.

After the feeding of the five thousand, Jesus perceived that the gratified and enthusiastic crowd wanted to take Him by force to make Him their king, so He departed again into a mountain alone, the disciples meanwhile going down to the sea to enter the boat. We notice first that Jesus declined their kingly offer. The average man would not have declined the crown, but Jesus Christ is not the average man; He is the sovereign Lord. He declined their offer of a crown because He knew the crown they wanted to give Him was not the crown He was destined to wear. Our Lord knew, also, that this was no time for the crown. He knew that there must be a cross out there before there could be a crown.

Now, we can be assured that our Lord Jesus Christ could never do the common thing, such as other men would do. To my mind, He is the supreme poet and artist and musician of all the world. All that is beautiful and lovely and gracious and desirable gather themselves up in our heavenly Bridegroom.

His birth was not a common birth, for our Lord stooped to mortal flesh to be born of the virgin Mary. He has, by the manner of His birth, elevated and dignified human birth beyond all possibilities of description.

The work He did was not common work, even though He humbled Himself to work at the carpenter's bench. What He did was to elevate all work and all labour up to an uncommon level and to dignify the most humble toil so that when the Christian carpenter saws and planes and pounds the nails he may know that he is doing an uncommon thing because our Lord, too, was a carpenter.

Jesus suffered when He was on earth, and yet His suffering was not the common, tight-lipped, cold-eyed suffering that goes on in our world. It was not that kind of suffering that has long ceased to find expression, not that suffering that destroys the higher regions of the spirit and bestialises us and makes us like the clay from which we came. The suffering of our Lord was uncommon because everything He did and said rose infinitely above the level of the common. If we are His now in faith, He has thus raised us all above the level of the common, so that we ourselves as children of God no longer do the common things. It is this elevation of things by the suffering Saviour that will explain why the most common act performed by the sinner brings no further thought, but becomes an extraordinary act when it is done by the believer in the spirit of Christ's compassion.

Our Lord also stooped to die, but His dying was not the common dying of a man. It was not the paying of a debt to nature, it was not the final payment on a mortgage that nature held over Him. No, nature never held a mortgage on Jesus Christ, for He never owed a dime to nature.

What made His death uncommon, unusual?

It was the dying of the just for the unjust. It was a sacrificial dying, it was a vicarious dying, it was the paying of a debt He did not owe for others who were too deeply in debt ever to pay out.

Being that kind of a Lord in His life and in His death, it is to be expected that His words were never common words. We understand well why His words never will be understood by the common man, that is, the ordinary rank and file of unconverted men, but we understand, too, why His words have always fallen like grace and truth upon the ears of the humble in heart and the meek in spirit.

Has not this been the testimony of all the saints of God down through the years? They have come to the flowers of the Scripture like bees, carrying away the sweet and precious nectar for their spiritual needs. But then, they have returned again and found that there was still as much nectar as there had been before. Like the barrel of meal that wasted not and the cruse of oil that did not fail, every text of Scripture, every word of our sovereign Lord, yields precious treasures no matter how often the visitation, no matter how acute the need.

So it was with the acts of Jesus. We see it in this lesson in the meaningful and significant act of our Lord in refusing the crown, and His withdrawal into the mountain. If He had stooped to receive the crown they wanted to give Him, Israel would have rallied to Him in a moment. But He took the cross in the will of God rather than to take a crown out of the will of God. What meaning, what direction there is for all of us here!

It takes some of us so long to learn for ourselves that the crown that comes before the cross is nothing but a tin crown. It is cheap and gilded, and if you would look, you would find an inscription stamped on it: 'Made in hell'. For it is not a crown that came down from the glory above, but a crown that came up from below, a false crown that came up 'Made in hell' for the soul that will take it before he takes the cross.

At the risk of repeating a religious cliché, I must point out that the will of God is always best, whatever the circumstances, and Jesus refused the crown and took the cross deliberately because it was in the will of God, both for Him and for humankind.

Brethren, let us not be afraid to take that cross and trust God for the crown. Why should so many in our day try to short-circuit their spiritual life and experience by eliminating the cross *en route* to the crown?

Let us apply this aspect of this event to our own selves and to our own time. Our Lord took the Father's will, escaped into the mountain, and His disciples saw Him go. And you know the New Testament story. He refused that crown that Israel wanted to give Him, and took the cross that the Romans gave Him. Then, on the third day, He arose from the dead, and then went upon Mount Olivet and ascended to the right hand of His Father's throne – not His own. And there He is today!

Now, what does Jesus do when He is in the mountain alone? What does any good man do when he is alone? He prays, of course. Jesus, that praying man of all praying men, that example of all praying men, was talking to His heavenly Father about the little group that He had just parted from a short time before – the disciples and those who had been fed and in their ignorance wanted to make Him their king.

By their human reckoning, He would bring about a revolution that would set Israel free, as in the days of Gideon and the great judges and prophets of the Old Testament. But Jesus knew them too well, and He knew that the worst thing He could do would be to put on a crown and bring those carnal folks into an earthly kingdom.

Actually, there would have to be many changes among them before they dared become sons and daughters of an earthly kingdom. So, He was praying for them in their ignorance and in their confusion, praying to the heavenly Father for His sheep – and that is exactly what He is doing now! Jesus is in heaven, praying for His people! I do not mean that our Lord is on His knees continually in the glory yonder, but He is in continual communion with the Father.

I remember years ago when dear old Dr Max Reich used to spend time with us, and he was asked at one time to describe his own prayer life. 'If you are asking me about getting alone and spending long periods alone on my knees, then I would have to say that I am relatively a prayerless man,' Dr Reich told us. 'But if you accept praying without ceasing as a continual, humble communion with God, day and night, under all circumstances, the pouring out of my heart to God in continual, unbroken fellowship – then I can say that I pray without ceasing!'

I believe that this is the manner in which our Lord is remembering us at the Father's throne, and His communion with the Father speaks to us of the necessity of a continual communion of our souls with God. This kind of communion and devotion does not consist of words.

I remember writing an editorial which I called 'Wordless Worship' in which I tried to present the idea that there is a worship that goes beyond human words. In fact, I have come to the conclusion that whatever can be put into words is second rate, for there are divine spiritualities that cannot be expressed. Remember, brethren if you can put it into words, it is second rate.

Paul called these divine spiritualities 'unspeakable', and they are the eternal things which do not pass away. It is here that we need to remember that God is allowing us to live on two planes at the same time. He lets us live on this religious plane where there are preachers and songleaders and choirs and pianists and organists and editors and leaders and promoters and evangelists, and that is religion. That is religion in overalls; that is the external garb of religion and it has its own place in God's work and plan. But, brethren, inside that and beyond that and above that and superior to all of the externals in our religious experience is the spiritual essence of it all – and it's that spiritual essence for which I am pleading, and which I want to see enthroned in our communion and fellowship in the church of Jesus Christ.

I have talked to you before about holding truth which begins and ends in itself, and the dangers of teaching and living so that truth is given no opportunity of moral expression.

We do have much theology, much Bible teaching and many Bible conferences which begin and end in themselves. They circle fully around themselves and after the benediction everyone goes home – but no one is any better than he was before. That is the woe and the terror of these things, my brethren. I plead for something more than textualism which begins and ends with itself, and sees nothing beyond.

If we do not see beyond the visible, and if we cannot touch that which is intangible, and if we cannot hear that which is not audible, and if we cannot know that which is beyond knowing, then I have serious doubts about the validity of our Christian experience. The Bible tells us that eye hath not seen nor ear heard, neither has it entered into the hearts of men the things that God has laid up for them that love Him.

That is why the apostle Paul goes on to remind us that God has revealed these mysteries to us by the Holy Spirit. Oh, my brethren, if we would only stop trying to make the Holy Spirit our servant and begin to live in His life as the fish lives in the sea, we would enter into the riches of glory about which we know nothing now.

There are too many who want the Holy Spirit in order that they may have the gift of healing. Others want the Holy Spirit for the gift of tongues. Others want Him to help them in the preaching ministry. Still others seek the Spirit that their testimony may become effective.

All of these things, I grant you, are a part of the total pattern of the New Testament, but it is impossible for us to make God our servant, and let us never pray that we may be filled with the Spirit of God for a secondary purpose. God wants to fill you with His Spirit as an end in your moral life. The purpose of God is that we should know Him first of all, and be lost in Him and that we should enter into the fullness of the Spirit that His Son may be glorified in us.

I try to read a good deal and bathe my soul in the writings and the hymns of the devoted saints of God who have lived in the centuries before us. These were men and women who lived and sang and dreamed and walked with God and were not for God took them, and they left behind such themes as 'Jesus, Thou Joy of Loving Hearts' and 'Jesus, the Very Thought of Thee, with Sweetness Fills My Breast.'

When I sense the shining glory of the life and works of many of God's choice saints of the past, I wonder why we ever stoop to read or sing or quote anything but that which is elevated and divine, noble and inspiring.

Jesus declined the crown, and went up into the mountain, and His presence there is actually the prayer. It is the fact of His presence. At the Father's throne, He is not everlastingly naming His people in pleading and in petition. He is not talking on and on, as some of us who are Christians do, covering our inward fears by our multitude of words. No, it is His presence at the right hand of the Father which constitutes His intercession for us. The fact that He is there is the might of His prayer, and that prayer is for His people – for you and me, and for the whole church of Jesus Christ.

In this drama, it is not difficult to envision the Christian church, for in the book of Acts, He had not more than reached the mountain yonder when suddenly the disciples were all filled with the Holy Spirit and the church of Christ was launched on the sea, on the dark sea, and she has been on that sea ever since.

When our Lord went up into the mountain and the clouds received Him out of their sight, the Light of the world went away, and night came. He had said, 'When I am with you, there is light, and it is daytime. But when I leave you and go away for a while, it will be night.'

It is so true that the night has settled on the world, and the church has worked in darkness throughout the years. I do not mean that the church has had no light, but I do say that the condition of the world has been darkness, and it has been as night upon the world throughout these centuries. The Dark Ages in history rightly should take in all of the time since the Sun of Righteousness withdrew, for it has been dark all over the world since He left the earth.

Let us consider the relationship of the ship to the sea. It is the relationship of propinquity and contact without merger – and that ought to be the relation of the church to the world. The world is the sea, the troubled sea that cannot rest. You will find in the Scriptures that when the world is used as a figure of speech, it means the sea, the disturbed, turbulent, treacherous, deadly, cruel sea. The sea can be so inviting and yet so unpredictable. It can be so calm today and so violent tomorrow. She bears her cargoes over her bosom in peace and tranquility today, but tomorrow she will dash them into the blue depths.

Mankind is like the sea in that respect. The leaders of the nations meet at conference tables and shake hands and exchange cigars and toast one another with their liquor. They have their pictures taken together; outwardly they laugh and joke as if in friendship. But the next day, war is declared, and these men are enemies and they would kill each other if given the chance. It is a turbulent, cruel, treacherous world in which we live. The world is real – and the Christian church is here in this world, and for a purpose. The church cannot withdraw from the world even as that tiny ship could not withdraw from the stormy sea.

So, we are here – the Christian church in this present world, but thank God, we are on top of it. We maintain the same relation to the world as did that little ship to the Sea of Tiberias. It is contact without merging.

The woe of it is this: the sea is always trying to get into the ship, and the world is always trying to get into the church. The world around us continues to try to find its way in, to splash in, to come in with soft words and beautiful white crests moving in on us, and always whispering, 'Don't be so aloof; don't be so hostile. Let us come in – we have something for you – something that will

do you good!' The world is making a lot of offers to the
church – but we don't need the world! Even some of my
friends lead me to believe that I stand pretty much alone
in all this. But I also know that I am telling a truth which
will stand when the world is on fire: that the world has
nothing that the Christian church needs!

I grant you that there is the sense of need which we have
because we are human beings and citizens. I get my starch
from the potato fields and my carbohydrates from the
stockyards and my milk from the cows and my eggs from
the hen. I travel on the highways of this world and fly in
her aeroplanes and ride on her trains, but that is another
thing altogether. Even in those things, we are not merging;
we are in contact without merging.

Some people say they are helped in their faith through
the offerings of science and the answers of education. I
have a little book in my study – I use it for a prop when I
want to get a little more air through the open window –
and it has chapters about Finding God Though Science,
Finding God Through Nature, Finding God Through Art.
Why should we be trying to find God through a backyard
window? Why should we always be peering out of some
cellar looking for God, when the whole top side of the
building is made of sheer crystal and God is shining down
– revealed! We need to open the windows of our hearts
and look up and invite Him into our lives.

I am sure that on that wildly stormy night when the sea
arose and hurled itself against the little boat, that the
disciples were busy with bailing, trying to keep the water
out. I cannot help but wonder whether, in the context of
our own day, two or three learned apostles would stand
by, and with superior knowledge and intellect, command:
'Stop bailing! Stop bailing! What you are doing belongs to
the seventeenth century. Your theology is a seventeenth
century theology. Why don't you get 'hep' and become
contemporary? You had better learn to become adjusted

to the world and the environment. Let the water come in – it won't hurt you.'

But, what about strong Peter with that bucket or container or whatever he was using? He was getting that water out of there as fast as he could. With him, it was a question of survival. And, whether we believe it or not, it is a question of survival with the church of Jesus Christ today!

It is not enough for the evangelical church to lean back on its forebears: 'We have Abraham for our father. Let us alone!' Jesus said in His day: 'Don't tell me that you have Abraham as your father. Look – the axe lies at the root of the tree, and if that tree is not bringing forth fruit, there will be someone to chop it down. But God will raise up another tree.'

The living God is not worried about our denominations and our churchly traditions – He is not pledged to preserve our denominational family trees. He only wants to get the world evangelised.

I confess that I didn't always have the vision to see this. I confess that many years ago I was perturbed because of a conversation I had with Dr Robert A. Jaffray, that great missionary statesman for Christ in the Far East. We were talking about The Christian and Missionary Alliance, the future of the church, and the future of the world. 'The preservation of The Alliance is of no great concern to God – that's not His business, at all!' Dr Jaffray told me. 'It is God's business to evangelise the world. Dissolve The Alliance if it is necessary, if we have to – but evangelise the world!'

I think I have that vision now: God is not busy and concerned about preserving any of our Christian denominations, but He is concerned about the life of the church of Jesus Christ – the spiritual church, regardless of what she may call herself. I think our Lord is concerned that the church of Jesus Christ should be saved from the

incoming waves. A little of the world here, a little there –
these move in on the church until the time comes when we
no longer have a spiritual church; we have a sinking
vessel.

In the context of this Bible lesson, we are told that the
disciples went down into the sea and that they were sailing
towards Capernaum and home. For them, Capernaum
was back home. So the disciples were in the ship on their
way home and it was night. In our day, the church of Jesus
Christ is on her way home, still toiling, still rowing, and it
is night.

When we think about the church, the real church of
God, the Body of Christ, some hold such an ideal picture
in their minds that it is hard for them to be realistic about
the toiling and the rowing. They think of the church in
idealistic terms – fixed up and garnished and made
beautiful in all ways.

But those disciples in the boat were not ideal men – they
were real men. They smelled of the sea. Their language
may not have been schooled and academic like Einstein's.
They were plain men who were sailing home, and there
was Another who was on the mountain praying for them
as they made the trip. There may have been some
disagreements in their conversations. Their situation was
not a perfect one and their talk was not sacred. There may
have been an argument. There may have been one of the
disciples who was in a mood to sulk along the way. One
man perhaps went to sleep and did not pull his part of the
load. Perhaps there were some who were better than
others on that ship that night – but they were all sailing
home together, and that other Presence was on the
mountain praying for them all.

So it is today in the real church of God. Not as in the
ideal, dream church of the hymns, but in the real church
of Christ – it is not a perfected church. I wish it were. If we
could find that perfect church, that perfect group, we

would all come crawling on hands and knees to ask for admittance, but we are a long way from being a perfect church.

There are still disagreements between the people of God – even among the saints of God. There were in Paul's day, and there are now. There are many imperfections among us. We may as well be realistic and call things by their right names. There are conditions that exist in the Christian churches which ought not to be there – but they are there. They are real.

What about it all in the sight of God? On the sea that night long ago, the disciples were tired and weary and sleepy and homesick, sailing for Capernaum and home. There situation was not ideal. They were still in human circumstances. But they were as the apple of His eye, and He loved them, and He prayed for them.

'It was now dark,' the Scripture says, 'and Jesus was not yet come.' My brethren, ought we not to be joining in confession and testimony: 'Oh, Lord Jesus, it is dark, and you have not come! It was dark in the first century, and the second, and you did not come. It was dark in the day of Constantine, and you did not come. It was dark when Bernard lived; it was dark when Luther preached, and it was dark when Wesley stood on his father's tombstone and preached, and you did not come. It was dark when George Fox walked up and down the hills and vales of England and you did not come. It is still dark, Lord, and we are not saying that we are disappointed, for we would not offend against the generation of Thy people, as David said.

'We don't want to admit that we are disappointed – but there is disappointment, nevertheless!'

Do you recall that when the World Council of Churches held its assembly in Evanston the delegates assembled from all over the world under the theme: 'Christ, the Hope of the World'? It was announced that there would be an emphasis on eschatology but they soon ran into a snag because of those in the Council who do not believe that the coming of Jesus Christ is the hope of the world. There was embarrassment when a leading Christian layman from London got up and said, 'Gentlemen, I believe that we ought to be preaching the Second Coming of Christ!' It was embarrassing for many of those old churchmen with their entrenched privileges and their vested interests and their robes and chains. They had the world by the tail and the church in their hand, and they were not ready to admit the necessity for the Lord to return to the earth.

In an earlier day, I am told, a Lutheran minister in Germany had an opportunity to preach in the hearing of Kaiser Wilhelm. It was before 1914, and the Kaiser got up in a blaze of anger and stared down the preacher who would dare to preach the imminent return of Jesus Christ. The return of Christ would have ruined the Kaiser's dream and plan of empire and conquest, and that is why some of those in leadership of the World Council were embarrassed: 'It would spoil our plans.'

Brethren, I do not want to be involved in any plans that would be spoiled if the Lord should return. Do you? I do not want to be caught with any secondary plans, any little schemes or dreams that have formed in my head. I want rather to fit into the plan of God, so that my activity would not be embarrassed or in any way disrupted if the Lord should come right now, walking on the sea!

It was dark, and no doubt they cried, 'Where are you, Lord?' as the tempest arose, and the great wind blew and tossed their ship.

Has not the Christian church prayed and worked and toiled through two great wars and a thousand revolutions in our own lifetime? I remember how the swift wind swept down in 1917 and they called it the Bolshevik revolution, when the royal rule was upset in Russia, and the

Communists took over. We have come through the dangers and the losses of another great world war, with the names of men rising and falling, the Hitlers, the Mussolinis, the Stalins, the Tojos. But the sabre-rattling will never end, whether it be in the Far East or the Near East, as long as the storm blows over the sea and the little ship is tossed about.

I know that the tempestuous wind is still sweeping over the surface of the deep, and I know that Christians are dying and their churches are being burned in some places. The big steel curtain and the bamboo curtain have been slammed in place, and our Christian brethren are behind them and they are cut off from us, entirely cut off. They cannot send out a carrier pigeon, nor a balloon carried by the winds. We do not have any word about that which is happening to the church in many places, in many lands.

But we know the godless doctines and we know the control, so we know what is happening. The tempest has caught the ship, and is trying to tear it apart, trying to break it up. But the church of Jesus Christ, composed of all the saints and the people of God, shall never perish!

We have Christ's promise that the gates of hell shall not prevail against His church. Churches may die, but *the* church must live. The church in Woochow may die, but *the* church still lives. The church in Colombia may have its pastor stoned and jailed and the people forced into hiding in the rocks and hills, but *the* church lives on. It is true that there is One in the mountain praying for *the* church, and He knows every one of His saints who has laid down his earthly life throughout the centuries because of his testimony and faith in Christ. Every one is safe in the bosom of the Lord Jesus Christ. There is a great wide garner into which the sheaves are taken, the golden sheaves of the spirit, and they will all shine in their Father's kingdom in that great day.

In the meantime, the church floats on the sea. While the

disciples row in their distress and danger, they see Jesus walking on the water. He could not remain away from them any longer. He had seen them and watched them all of that time with the eyes that never close. They were held in His hand, and they did not know it.

Brethren, I remind you that Jesus Christ is still the Lord. He is still the head of His Body, the church. We do not have to apologise for Him; He does not want us to soften His gospel to make it more acceptable to the world. He is not looking for us to defend Him, to argue on His behalf. He is still in charge. His eyes see through the fog and the night. He holds the church in the hollow of His hand even while it is being tossed on the wild sea.

At the proper time, when He was desperately needed, He left the mountain and hurried down and walked on the water, approaching the little craft.

Are we clean enough and pure enough and honest enough and so thoroughly and genuinely His that we can see Him and hear Him? He is not here yet – but He is coming! He is walking on our stormy sea. He is approaching the ship. We do not know when He will come within hailing distance, but we know He will come at just the right time. His love and His keen interest in His people will not permit Him to stay any longer at the right hand of God the Father Almighty than is necessary.

With all that is within me, I believe that the Lord Jesus Christ, the Sovereign, walks on the sea. He is the Sovereign Lord – and how different from the kings and rulers of the earth who claim to be sovereign, but their lands and territories and empires are all marked out by boundaries.

The word 'sovereign' means absolute, infinite, unqualified ruler in all realms, in heaven and earth and sea – and that is what our Lord is. In His providential plan, He imposes certain limitations upon Himself for a little while, that He may fulfil His eternal purposes and destinies. At any moment, He can walk upon the waters of the earth or the fires of hell or the golden streets of heaven – for He is the Sovereign Lord!

Our risen and glorified Saviour, Jesus Christ, takes no orders from anyone. He has no counsellors to call in for star chamber sessions. He has no assistant lord, He has no secretary to the throne, He needs no one upon whom to lean, He needs no one from whom to seek advice. He knows in one effortless act all that can be known and He has already lived out all of our tomorrows and holds the world in the palm of His hand.

That is the Lord I serve. I gladly own that I am His. Glory be to God – the Christ we know is infinitely beyond all men and all angels and all seraphim and cherubim; above all archangels and all principalities and powers and might and dominion and things visible and invisible – for He is the origin of them all!

So, He walks on the sea. Let us not be fearful, brethren. Some worry about the nation, some worry about their jobs, some fret about the stock markets, some see the spectre of another depression. All of this time there are wars and rumours of wars. We ought to be ashamed as the children of God, the disciples of Christ, the members of the Body of Christ, His church, if we are frightened. He is walking on the sea, and He is coming our way, and our little ship is on its way home, though it is dark and the winds blow strong.

He is our Sovereign Lord! This is the wonder of it all – He is waiting to be wanted. He is waiting to be invited in!

# Whatever Happened to Worship?

## by A. W. Tozer

This is the book A. W. Tozer intended to write next. Now, more than twenty years after he was called home to heaven, it is available—compiled from tapes of sermons preached to his congregations in Toronto.

'True worship,' says Tozer, 'is to be so personally and hopelessly in love with God, that the idea of a transfer of affection never even remotely exists.'

A joint publication

 *STL Books and Kingsway Publications* k̆

# The Divine Conquest

## by A. W. Tozer

'The essentiality of a right interior life was the burden of Christ's teaching, and was without doubt one of the main causes of His rejection of those notorious externalists, the Pharisees. Paul also preached continually the doctrine of the indwelling Christ, and history will reveal that the Church has gained or lost power exactly as she has moved toward or away from the inwardness of her faith.'

*(from the author's Preface)*

In a day when there are so many confusing currents in the church, Dr Tozer points the way forward to inner spiritual reality and power.

A joint publication

*STL Books and Kingsway Publications* k

# Leaning into the Wind

## by A. W. Tozer

What is the way ahead for the church? What does renewal really involve? Are we ready for revival?

These and other related issues are dealt with uncompromisingly by Dr Tozer in this volume. According to Tozer, Christians must choose between easy conversions – or saintliness; entrenchment – or trust in the Spirit; big business methods – or New Testament principles; compromise – or a strong resolve to follow God even though it takes all our strength to resist other forces and 'lean into the wind'.

'Here are . . . words to wound but not destroy, designed as a clarion call for God's people to return to long forsaken positions in order to regain the ground that has been so easily lost.'
*Clive Calver.*

A joint publication

 *STL Books and Kingsway Publications* k

# The Pursuit of God

**by A. W. Tozer**

'This book is a modest attempt to aid God's hungry children so to find Him. Nothing here is new except in the sense that it is a discovery which my own heart has made of spiritual realities most delightful and wonderful to me. Others before me have gone much farther into these holy mysteries than I have done, but if my fire is not large it is yet real, and there may be those who can light their candle at its flame.'

*(from the author's Preface)*

A joint publication

*STL Books and Kingsway Publications* k